I0303845

Chinua Achebe: New Perspectives

Umelo Ojinmah

Spectrum Books Limited
Ibadan • Owerri • Kaduna

Published by
Spectrum Books Limited
Sunshine House
Second Commercial Road
Oluyole Estate
Ibadan, Nigeria

in association with
Safari Books (Export) Limited
Bel Royal House
Hilgrove Street
St. Helier, Jersey
Channel Islands, UK

© Umelo Ojinmah 1991

All rights reserved. No part of this publication may be reproduced, stored in a retrieval system or transmitted in any form or by any means, electronic, mechanical, electrostatic, magnetic tape, photocopying, recording or otherwise, without the prior written consent of the author who is the copyright owner.

First Published 1991

ISBN 978-246-116-4

Printed by Intec Printers Limited, Ibadan

To my wife, Simbo, and those others whose love and goodwill made this work possible

List of Abbreviations

MYCD	Chinua Achebe, *Morning Yet on Creation Day*
AMOP	Chinua Achebe, *A Man of the People*
TFA	Chinua Achebe, *Things Fall Apart*
AOG	Chinua Achebe, *Arrow of God*
NLE	Chinua Achebe, *No Longer at Ease*
Anthills	Chinua Achebe, *Anthills of the Savannah*
GAW	Chinua Achebe, *Girls at War and Other Stories*
B S B	Chinua Achebe, *Beware Soul Brother*
Awoonor	Kofi Awoonor, *The Breast of the Earth*
Ravenscroft	Arthur Ravenscroft, *Chinua Achebe*
McEwan	Neil McEwan, *Africa and the Novel*
Taiwo	Oladele Taiwo, *Culture and the Nigerian Novel*
Killam	GD Killam, *Novels of Chinua Achebe*
Gakwandi	S A Gakwandi, *The Novel and Contemporary Experience in Africa*
Moore	Gerald Moore, *Seven African Writers*
Palmer	Eustace Palmer, *An Introduction to the West African Novel*

Contents

Introduction	vi

Chapter One
The Seer as Custodian of Regenerative Wisdom in Traditional Society: Achebe's View of the Role of the African Writer ... 1

Chapter Two
The Manifestation of Abuse of Power in Achebe's Early Fiction ... 11

Chapter Three
A Legacy Squandered: Achebe's Disillusionment at Post-colonial Irresponsibility in *No Longer at Ease* and *A Man of the People* ... 35

Chapter Four
The Unwanted Seer: Achebe's Short Stories, Poems of War and Recent Fiction ... 76

Conclusion ... 106
Notes ... 110
Bibliography ... 119

Introduction

The writings of Chinua Achebe are so realistic, so correlatively true to life, that in analysing them one is tempted to forget that they essentially are works of fiction. An objective appreciation of contemporary happenings in society only heightens one's apprehension of the social realism of these works, for they really mirror contemporary society. It is this, more than anything else, that accounts for the continued relevance of these writings. This is not to say that without such relevance the works can be discountenanced, because any such averment will be erroneous. On their individual merits as works of literature, each of Achebe's writings can pass through any analytical crucible and emerge as fine works of art.

Achebe in his analysis of governance in our part of the world states that:

> The trouble... was that none of us had been indoors long enough to be able to say "To hell with it." We had all been in the rain together until yesterday. Then a handful of us -- the smart and the lucky and hardly ever the best -- had scrambled for the one shelter our former rulers left, and had taken it over and barricaded themselves in. And from within they had sought to persuade the rest, through numerous loudspeakers, that the first phase of the struggle had been won and that the next phase -- the extension of our house -- was even more important and called for new and original tactics; it required that all argument should cease and the whole people speak with one voice and that any more dissent and argument outside the door of the shelter would subvert and bring down the whole house.
>
> (AMOP, p.42)

This book attempts to look at the themes: power and responsibility which Achebe seems to be obsessed with, particularly as they affect political governance in Africa. *Chinua Achebe: New Perspectives* trade these themes from *Things Fall Apart* through the essays, to *Anthills of the Savannah* in a way that is bound to revolutionise the thinking of many scholars and students of the writings of Chinua Achebe. For example, many readers of Achebe's *Things Fall Apart* and *Arrow of God* hold the view that Okonkwo and Ezeulu are representative of their societies and that both are destroyed defending the society. But that is not so. It is the contention of this book that the afflictions of the post-colonial African societies with irresponsible leaders were already manifest in the colonial period, through characters such as Okonkwo and Ezeulu, whom Achebe sees as guilty of gross abuse of power and privilege. Achebe's belief that the African writer in contemporary society should help educate his society, reclaim its traduced past heritage, be its critic and mentor, is well known. However, Achebe maintains that one can neither do this, nor have a meaningful future without having a proper sense of our historical past, and one's position in it. The reality in positing for a reclamation of a society's past heritage, Achebe realised, was that some of the post-colonial tensions of his people originate from an incomplete apprehension of all the aspects of this heritage, and the lack of understanding of the responsibility that power imposes on those who exercise it:

> In the beginning Power rampaged through the world, naked. So the Almighty . . . decided to send his daughter, Idemili, to bear witness to the moral nature of authority by wrapping around Power's rude waist a loincloth of peace and modesty.
>
> *(AOG,* p. 102)

In Achebe's view, the main problem in contemporary Nigerian society, as well as in many independent African societies, is the lack of restraint in wielding power, added to an unbridled scramble for materialism, which in most cases result in the destruction of democratic principles. Achebe, therefore, believes that the only viable solution to the society's post-colonial tensions is a re-formation of the inherited cultural values around society's traditional world-view.

One cannot but agree that it is no more enough to blame outsiders for our woes, to stridently repeat the refrain of colonialism and its aftermath, rather than face squarely the responsibilities which self governance imposes. According to Philip Rogers, Achebe's poem, "Lazarus", in which Ogbaku people kill their kinsman "on the threshold of a promising resurrection", elicits intense sense of disillusionment and of betrayal, for "the moment of birth is blighted, but the blighting force can no longer be dismissed as external". Having noted the total aversion to criticism, whether positive or negative, which is prevalent among those in positions of power in contemporary African societies, Achebe nevertheless, would rather roll out the "talking drum" than gnash his teeth in mute acquiescence. As Kim Heron notes:

> Achebe's vision of the sort of artist/critic that the contemporary society needs as against the one that had always operated in

traditional society is compounded by the fascist oriented governments within which such contemporary artists have to work. Modern societies in which the freedom of criticism has functioned in traditional societies is curtailed by blatant intimidations and draconian decrees, and often physical incarcerations: "Mr Achebe said his relations with authorities are strained. He went home in December to accept an honorary doctorate from the state university at Lagos, for example; the ceremony was abruptly called off . . . 'It's risky and dangerous, this kind of love-hate relationship with authorities, he said, 'but I really have no choice in the matter. I would be very, very sad to have to live in Europe or America (exile)."

Chinua Achebe: New Perspectives has been written with the intention of eliciting certain fundamental messages embedded in Achebe's works, and with the hope that we can now afford to stop playing the ostrich. Ngugi Wa Thiong'o sums up this analysis, saying: "The teacher no longer stands apart to contemplate. He has moved with a whip among the pupils, flagellating himself as well as them", and as will be plain by the new perspective adopted in this work, Ngugi further makes the point that: "What Achebe has done in [both] *A Man of the People* [and *Anthills of the Savannah*] is to make it impossible or inexcusable for other African writers to do other than address themselves directly to their audiences in Africa . . . and tell them that such problems are their concern."

A toast to a new beginning.

U.R.Ojinmah

CHAPTER ONE

The Seer as Custodian of Regenerative Wisdom in Traditional Society: Achebe's View of the Role of the African Writer

Many scholars and critics of Achebe's writings acknowledge, as Achebe does, the didactic nature of his writings from *Things Fall Apart* to *Anthills of the Savannah*. Fundamental to this didacticism is Achebe's stated intent to preserve the traditional role of the artist in many indigenous African societies as both the custodian of the people's customs and traditions and proponent of its regenerative wisdom, without which the society, often, is doomed. Underlying this objective has been the engaged dialectics of the responsibility which power imposes on its possessors. A fact which the ancients recognised and which traditional society appreciated and demanded of those whom it placed in positions of power, and which disregard accounts, in many cases, for the incessant misrules and abberrations that plague many post-colonial new nations of Africa and elsewhere.

Achebe's writings attempt to convey this responsibility and the effects and consequences of its disregard on contemporary post-colonial societies. Before proceeding further, it is necessary to establish the circumstances that have conditioned Achebe's writing career. Achebe himself has written about the early influences that spurred him to become a writer, and what he sees as the writer's primary functions in contemporary African societies. He has several times said that reading Joyce Cary's *Mister Johnson* among other works of the period made him realise, "that the story we had to tell could not be told for us by anyone else no matter how well gifted or well-intentioned."[1] In

an interview with Lewis Nkosi in 1962, Achebe, elaborating on this, says:
> I was quite certain I was going to try my hand at writing, and one of the things that set me thinking was Joyce Cary's novel set in Nigeria, *MrJohnson*, which was praised so much, and it was clear to me that this was a most superficial picture of, not only of the country, but even of the Nigerian character and so I thought if this was famous, then perhaps someone ought to try and look at this from the inside.[2]

Achebe also mentions that he has always been interested in stories: "I have always been fond of stories and intrigued by language - first Igbo, spoken with such eloquence by the old men of the village, and later English which I began to learn at about the age of eight;"*(MYCD*,p.67). Coupled with this was Achebe's "fascination for the ritual and the life" of the non-Christian neighbours of his childhood (*(MYCD*, p.68).

In his answer to one of Lewis Nkosi's questions in the interview mentioned above Achebe says: "Well things are changing very fast but if one is interested, one can still see signs of what life used to look like."[3] The implication of this is that Achebe, in writing, was aiming at preserving "what life used to look like" and to tell "their story" from the perspective of an indigenous African. As Philip Rogers notes: "Each of Achebe's four novels has had an obvious (but never obtrusive) purpose.*Things Fall Apart* and*Arrow of God* both aim to show that the African [had a] past."[4] It could be argued that this act of preservation of the past is in consonance with his stated role of teaching, for Achebe grew up at a period when Anglophone school children were fed a diet of English literature that most felt they did not relate to culturally: "In those days the new British-style universities in Africa were intended to transplant into African soil what established academic circles in England regarded as the best features of English universities, without much regard for the special needs of the countries where they were set up."[5] This was a period which also saw the traumatic results on the African psyche of decades of European calumniation of their cultural and religious heritages:
> When I was a schoolboy it was unheard of to stage Nigerian dances at any of our celebrations. We were told and we believed that our dances were heathen. The Christian and proper thing to do was for the boys to drill with wooden swords and the girls to perform, of all things, Maypole dances. Beautiful clay bowls and

pots were only seen in the homes of the heathen. We civilized Christians used cheap enamel-ware from Europe and Japan; instead of water pots we carried kerosine cans. In fact, to say that a product was Ibo-made was to brand it with the utmost inferiority. When a people have reached this point in their loss of faith in themselves their detractors need do no more; they have made their point.[6]

One of the results of this sort of attitude was what Achebe sees as manifest "self-contempt" which leads the African into believing that they are inferior to all other races, and for which he states: "If I were God I would regard as the very worst our acceptance - for whatever reason - of racial inferiority "(MYCD, p.44).

Chinua Achebe is most forthright when he delves into what he believes the role of a writer, particularly an African writer, to be. Many critics have made much of Achebe's essay, "The Novelist as Teacher", in which he makes mention of a boy in his wife's class who was ashamed of writing about the harmattan because he was afraid that the other boys would ridicule him and writes:

> It is my business as a writer to teach that boy that there is nothing disgraceful about the African weather, that the palm-tree is a fit subject for poetry. Here then is an adequate revolution for me to espouse -- to help my society regain belief in itself and put away the complexes of the years of denigration and self-abasement. And it is essentially a question of education, in the best sense of that word. Here, I think, my aims and the aspirations of my society meet . . . . I would be quite satisfied if my novels (especially the ones I set in the past) did no more than teach my readers that their past -- with all its imperfections -- was not one long night of savagery from which the Europeans acting on God's behalf delivered them.
>
> (*MYCD*, pp.44-5)

The above factors have had the cumulative effect of sharpening Achebe's social consciousness. And it is this social consciousness, Cairns says, that informs Achebe's writings: "In that his political and philosophical stance so consciously informs his novels, Achebe's 'applied art' continues the tradition of the old-time Ibo artists. The productions of these artists were functional and utilitarian, with a clearly defined place in the social and spiritual life of the entire community."[7] Achebe is

adamant about the African writer's relationship to his society, as Rogers notes:
> In Chinua Achebe's view, the African writer of our time must be accountable to his society; if he fails to respond to the social and political issues of his age, to espouse the 'right and just causes' of his people, he is no better than 'the absurd man in the proverb who deserts his burning house to pursue a rat fleeing from the flames.[8]

For Achebe, the African novelist as teacher has three primary functions in relation to his society: as historian, rescuing its past; as a critic, analysing its present; as mentor, helping to guide it towards its future.

In Achebe's view the African writer's first task is to rescue the African past from the colonial misrepresentation and biased stereotyping to which it had been subjected. Kofi Awoonor writes that: "Achebe's *Things Fall Apart* seems to have been inspired by a need to respond to what seemed to be Cary's sniggering laugh at Africa, whose image of filed teeth and bones stuck in the nose has scarcely receded in the Europe of Cary's colonial experience."[9] Continuing, he notes that:
> To Achebe, the African world before the arrival of Europe was a well-integrated one, with dignity and honour . . . . As a story of the tragic encounter between Africa and Europe, *[Things Fall Apart]* is an attempt to capture and restate the pristine integrity which has been so traumatically shattered by that confrontation.
> (Awoonor,p.252)

In Achebe's views, the artist -- writer, carver, composer, or dancer-- in contemporary African societies has to perform the dual function of educating his audience and helping them reclaim their past heritage. As he says, these artists like their historian counterparts, have the necessary function of "replacing short, garbled, despised history with more sympathetic account . . . because we must begin to correct the prejudices which generations of detractors created about the Negro."[10] This, he sees as a necessary step before any meaningful progress:
> This is my answer to those who say that a writer should be writing about contemporary issues -- about politics in 1964, about the last *coup d'état*. Of course, these are all legitimate themes for a writer but as far as I am concerned the fundamental theme must first be disposed of. This theme -- put quite simply -- is that African people did not hear of culture for the first time from Europeans, that their societies were not mindless but frequently had a philosophy of great depth and value and beauty, that they had poetry, and, above all, they had dignity. It is this dignity that

many African people all but lost during the colonial period, and it is this that they must now regain.[11]

Achebe goes on elsewhere to say that: "The writer cannot expect to be excused from the task of re-education and regeneration that must be done. In fact he should march right in front" (*MYCD*, p.45). He believes that in performing these functions the contemporary artist will only be following in the footsteps of their ancestors in traditional African societies: "Our ancestors created their myths and legends and told their stories for a human purpose . . . .Their artists lived and moved and had their being in society, and created their works for the good of that society" (*MYCD*,p.19). But the writer, Achebe says, must provide a view of this past (both colonial and early post-colonial past) which is not romanticised, but which is authentic and takes into consideration what he terms the "human condition" (*MYCD*, p.24).

The African writer must not only rescue his society's past, but must also be a commentator on its present course. Achebe believes that the writer has to be a free critic in a society lacking such criticism. On this Chukwudi Maduka writes that to Achebe as to "most of the African writers . . . there is a direct relationship between literature and social institutions.The principal function of literature is to criticise these institutions and eventually bring about desirable changes in the society."[12] It is pertinent to note that this function of social criticism, in Achebe's view, has to be for the benefit of that society. An example of this social consciousness and the over-riding impulse for "the good of the community" which informs his writings is seen in the preface to Achebe's book of essays, *Morning Yet on Creation Day*, with its overt comment on public interest being an essential criterion to the resolution of any artist's doubts in his creation. Reacting to a widespread sentiment in the years following the Nigerian Civil War, 1967-1970, that the recent past was best forgotten, Achebe says:

> I do not agree. I believve that in our situation the greater danger lies not in remembering but in forgetting, in pretending that slogans are the same as truth; and that Nigeria, always prone to self-deception, stands in great need of reminders . . . . I believe that if we are to survive as a nation we need to grasp the meaning of tragedy. One way to do it is to remind ourselves constantly of the things that happened and how we felt when they were happening.
> (*MYCD*, p.xiii)

This function of social criticism is the least expounded part of Achebe's exposition of the artist's role in traditional African societies, and he sees it as a direct extension of the function of a teacher, namely, to chastise. Achebe acknowledges this not so pleasing but necessary aspect of the teacher's role when he tells other African writers that "we must seek the freedom to express our thought and feeling, even against ourselves, without the anxiety that what we say might be taken in evidence against our race."[13] He believes that contemporary African writers ought to seek out and criticise corruption and all forms of evil in the society without pausing to consider whether such criticisms will become ammunition for their detractors. Adrian Roscoe says, in discussing the above comment by Achebe, that: "The feeling of forever standing before a tribunal must be discarded."[14]

Achebe sees this extension and application of the writer's role as important because in traditional African societies the two roles, that of critic and social commentator, are merged. Achebe's teachings, which are often scathing, presuppose the duty of chastisement as an integer of the role of a teacher. If the African writer should influence his society's perception and sense of direction, Achebe argues that he should have "a proper sense of history" and most importantly he should tell his society "where [they] went wrong, where the rain began to beat [them]" (*MYCD*, p.44). This is a function which Achebe believes has already been abdicated in contemporary African societies by those whose duty it rightly is as in other modern societies, the press:

> Those who enter politics do so mainly out of self-interest; those who actively comment on the political scene, the journalists, are also clearly seeking their own interests in their manner of reporting political incidents. The mass of the people who are caught in the turbulence of politics are easily swayed and as easily erupt into violent action. The press is resented but has to be stilled by bribery.[15]

Achebe puts it more bluntly through Chief Nanga in *A Man of the People*: "If I don't give him something now, tomorrow he will go and write rubbish about me. They say it is the freedom of the Press. But to me it is nothing short of freedom to crucify innocent men and assassinate their character .... I don't say they should not criticize - after all no one is perfect except God - but they should criticise constructively"(*AMOP*,p.74). To Achebe, then, freedom of the press represents an essential precondition for the existence of a meaningful democratic governance: "It is generally an unspoken assumption in discussion about the press . . . that it is in some sense a bastion of democracy, a safeguard against the various assaults which are made on democracy."[16] Achebe finds this function of the press comparable to the functioning in traditional village in African societies of consensus, where every adult male is entitled to contribute to debates on issues of concern to the whole society.

As historian of his society's past and critic of its present state, the African writer, Achebe believes, should not be a passive observer and recorder but should help form a vision of the future direction of his society. In the words of René Wellek, literature is a "reflection of reality" and provides the "truest mirror . . . if the author shows an insight into the structure of the society and the future direction of its evolution".[17] Achebe's social consciousness is heightened by this general belief, as noted by Chukwudi Maduka, which seems to pervade the African literary scene that: "Literature can play a great role in straightening the patterns of social change in Africa "(Maduka, p.13). Quoting Kofi Awoonor of Ghana, he argues, as Chinua Achebe does, that if the writer "has to provide a vision for those who are going to order his society . . .he must be a person who has some kind of conception of the society in which he is living and the way he wants the society to go"(Maduka,p.13). This parallels Achebe's views in his interview with Bernth Lindfors in which he states:

> Yes, I think by recording what had gone on before, they [the African writers] were in a way helping to set the tone of what was going to happen. And this is important because at this stage it seems to me that the writer's role is more in determining than merely reporting. In other words, his role is to act rather than to react . . . . 'Let us map out what we are going to be tomorrow.' I think our most meaningful job today should be to determine what kind of society we want, how we are going to get there, what values we can take from the past, if we can, as we move along.[18]

He further states that "a writer in the African revolution who steps aside can only write footnotes or glossary when the event is over."[19] This again is reflected in Maduka's statement that: "The African writer cannot afford the luxury of withdrawing into the cocoon of creativity in the name of art for art's sake. As a participant in the drama of social change in Africa, he can use his skills to help shape the future of the society"(Maduka, p.13).

Achebe's writings highlight the above commitments and motivations. Those set in the past espouse the African cultural heritage while his more recent writings have aimed at ascertaining "where we went wrong, where the rain began to beat us" as a prerequisite to "knowing where to begin to dry ourselves." But in all his writings, Achebe has been consistent in the role he has chosen to play - that of the teacher. He has not spared the rod as an instrument of chastisement where necessary. Achebe has seen it as necessary sometimes to change the focus and direction of his message but the fundamentals have always been consistent and intact: "Having fought with the nationalist movements and been on the side of the politicians, I realized after independence that they and I were now on different sides, because they were not doing what we had agreed they should do. So I became a critic .... I was still doing my job as a writer .... I think what you do as a writer depends on the state of your society."[20] It is this social consciousness and the added complication of a civil war (the result of the nationalists not doing what they agreed they should do) that induced the hiatus in Achebe's literary career which will be discussed later.

It is my contention, therefore, that in spite of Chinua Achebe's remarks in his essay, "Colonialist Criticism", about European critical perception concerning "the African and responsibility", that he perceives the evasion and shirking of responsibility, as central to the resolution of his people's post-colonial tensions.[21] In Achebe's view, this is particularly important if meaningful democratic governance is to eventuate in African new states.

Contrary to his own critical views in "Colonialist Criticism", Achebe sees much of the post-colonial tensions in African new states and their resolution as consequent on the disregard by individuals in positions of power of the responsibility which such positions and power imposes. While he believes that it is probably all right to apportion blame and point accusatory fingers at the evils and disruptions wrought by colonialism, he is also of the view that the African has not fared better at the hands of the post-colonial black administrative class. Coupled with the above views, on responsibility and governance, is a firm belief that a critical appraisal of Achebe's writings from the perspective that I have adopted will elucidate a more detailed perception of the writer's views on "how we have fared in the post-colonial period", his disillusionments and the reasons for them, and particularly what he sees as the solution. It is my considered opinion that Achebe sees a fundamental reason for some of the post-colonial tensions as being the absolute lack of responsibility, restraint, and tolerance that necessarily go with democratic governance of any form: family, village, clan, or country. It becomes necessary at this juncture to define my use of the term -- responsibility, and its relevance and application. Frequently when the term "responsible" is used in African societies, it is applied so as to distinguish between right and wrong. This book's interest in this definition of responsibility is only peripheral, for it is on its other definitions (as meaning "accountable", "answerable", "deserving credit or blame for stewardship", "reliable", and "an ability to meet obligations", especially moral ones), that this analysis focuses. Neal Ascherson in his review of Achebe's *Anthills of the Savannah* makes much the same point:

> In his new novel, his first since A Man of the People (1966), Chinua Achebe says, with implacable honesty, that Africa itself is to blame [for the corruption, mismanagement, collapse of democracy], and that there is no safety in excuses that place the fault in the colonial past or in the commercial and political manipulations of the First World. The first postcolonial leaders, for all their European educations and sophistication, utterly failed to meet their responsibility. And by the time that they began to understand the scale of their failure, their own brief period of hegemony was beginning to fall apart as power passed into the hands of more limited and infinitely more ferocious men, usually military . . . . It is a tale about responsibility, and the ways in which men who should know better betray and evade that responsibility.[22]

While one notes Achebe's call that African writers and critics should ". . . emulate those men of Benin, ready to guide the curious visitor to the gallery of their art, willing to listen with politeness even to his hasty opinions but careful, most careful, to concede nothing to him that might appear to undermine their own position within their heritage or compromise the integrity of their indigenous perception", it is equally of primary importance that a perceptive analysis of his writings should elucidate those lessons of history which he seems so anxious to teach and should take cognizance of all facets of the inherent truth in those writings (*MYCD*, p.18).

Achebe's writings fall into two broad categories. The first, those set in the past -*Things Fall Apart* (1958) and *Arrow of God* (1964) both examine a particular cultural world-view prior to, and immediately preceding the advent of Europeans. The second, includes *No Longer at Ease* (1960), *A Man of the People* (1966), his book of short stories, *Girls at War* (1972), and his latest novel, *Anthills of the Savannah* (1987), which are set in the present and deal with contemporary Nigeria. This book proffers the argument that Achebe's writings typify his people's response to their post-colonial tensions, and intends to show what Achebe believes to be their post-colonial tensions and the solution. It will particularly highlight Achebe's persistent probing of the issues of abuse of power and irresponsibility as reflected in his novels, and the centrality of these issues to the overall theme of his people's post-colonial tensions. In doing so, I intend to divide his writings into two broad categories - those set in the past and the ones set in the present. Instead of basing my analysis on the chronological order in which his books are written, the arrangement will be based on the time and chronology of events. This, therefore, means that *Arrow of God* will come immediately after *Things Fall Apart*, rather than after *No Longer at Ease*. While *A Man of the People* will follow *No Longer at Ease*, rather than *Arrow of God*.

CHAPTER TWO

The Manifestation of Abuse of Power in Achebe's Early Fiction

Things Fall Apart: Okonkwo: an Embodiment of Ibo Traditional Values and its Excesses, and Okonkwo the Deviant

Achebe believes that for contemporary African societies to make any meaningful progress, they have to establish concrete links with their past. In considering the first category of his fiction, those set in the past, and the fundamental messages that have given rise to his present disillusionment, it becomes necessary to observe from the outset that this belief has not changed: "But what I mean is that owing to the peculiar nature of our situation it would be futile to try to take off before we have repaired our foundations. We must first set the scene which is authentically African, then what follows will be meaningful and deep."[1] This is because Achebe sees a people's apprehension of their world as reflective of their general perception of life, and their place in it.

Most readers and critics of Achebe's early writings agree that in *Things Fall Apart* Achebe aims to show the African society before the coming of the European. Critics such as G.D.Killam, Adrian Roscoe, Eldred Jones, and Kofi Awoonor among others, also acknowledge that in recreating the Ibo society of his grandfather's generation, Achebe paints a very realistic portrait of this people. Killam writes that:

> Things Fall Apart is a vision of what life was like in Iboland between 1850 and 1900. Achebe makes a serious attempt to capture realistically the strains and tensions of the experiences of Ibo people under the impact of colonialism. What ultimately gives this novel its strength is Achebe's feelings for the plight and the problems of these peoples.[2]

Achebe shows through an exposé of their daily routine and the complex nature of the interactions between individuals, with their gods, and their society, a deep awareness and understanding of the structural complexity of even the simplest societal organisation. Such social activities as inter-village wrestling matches become avenues of cultural exposition:

> The drums were still beating, persistent and unchanging. Their sound was no longer a separate thing from the living village. It was like the pulsation of its heart. It throbbed in the air, in the sunshine, and even in the trees, and filled the village with excitement.... The whole village turned out on the *ilo*, men, women and children.
>
> (*TFA*, pp.40-2)

Even family affairs such as marriages highlight the communal nature of the society's life. Such occasions not only afford both villages (the suitor's village and the woman's village)[3] an opportunity of interacting socially, but also to examine and compare the different customs of the various neighbouring clans, and consequently theirs:

> As the men ate and drank palm-wine they talked about the customs of their neighbours."It was only this morning," said Obierika, "that Okonkwo and I were talking about Abame and Aninta, where titled men climb trees and pound foo-foo for their wives".... "All their customs are upside-down. They do not decide bride-price as we do, with sticks; they haggle and bargain as if they were buying a goat or cow in the market." 'That is very bad".... "But what is good in one place is bad in another place."
>
> (*TFA*, pp.66-7)

As Awoonor says, Achebe's exposition is realistic for he recreates a society that is "governed by its well-tried mores, laws, sanctions, taboos, is well integrated, a living structure, an organism animated with the life and movement of its members and gods"(Awoonor,p.253).

Things Fall Apart thus symbolised for Achebe the beginning of this restoration and repair of "our foundations". Achebe's account and historical perspective is realistic, for despite his proclaimed goal, Awoonor acknowledges that, "As a man who set out to redress the balance and tell the African side of the story, he [Achebe] has done more than a propagandist's hack job" (Awoonor, p.280). *Things Fall Apart* also sets out to correct assumptions that Africa is an historically barren landscape, both in the eyes of its detractors, Achebe says, and also in the eyes of its people themselves: "A writer who feels the need to right this wrong cannot escape the conclusion that the past needs to be recreated not only for the enlightenment of our detractors but even more for our own education."[4]

Achebe portrays Umuofia of *Things Fall Apart* as a pluralistic society which admires energetic, aggressive and ambitious members, one that is patient, tolerant and forbearing, entrenched in the wisdom of its ancients, yet flexible and adaptable when necessary. This is a society which, in Achebe's view, is not given to rashness, particularly as "its Oracle never sends it out to do battle in an unjust cause" (*TFA*, p.12). While the society extols the virtues that Okonkwo cultivates, its dynamic lies in its flexibility. Achebe shows that this society is accommodative. David Carroll makes the point that:, "This open form of society is also very susceptible to outside influence, always ready to examine new ideas, . . . adaptable in the extreme if it finds these ideas acceptable."[5] Arthur Ravenscroft observes that through Achebe's vivid presentation of the elaborate rituals of the society's life, "the impression emerges of a carefully ordered yet flexible culture, communal in nature yet allowing for a considerable measure of individuality."[6] And as Carroll further remarks, "the flexible, non-authoritarian system fosters and is fostered by the highly individualistic temperament of the Igbo"(Carroll, p.16). This society is like Achebe's Onitsha which "sees everything", and because of its belief that its survival as a social organisation lies in its flexibility, it "has come to distrust single-mindedness"(*MYCD*, p.91). It is in this flexibility or lack of it that the difference between Okonkwo and his society lies: "Okonkwo aims to embody every virtue of his clan but he fails to achieve the balance and caution valued by his culture."[7]

But Achebe does not only portray the virtues of the society, he also shows the society simultaneously practising superstitious beliefs. These include the practice of viewing twins as

portending evil, and of throwing them into the Evil Forest to die, human sacrifices, and exaggerated shows of manliness, such as when tribal members drink publicly from the human skulls of their first victims during certain ceremonies. Oladele Taiwo writes of Achebe's fiction, thus:
> Besides the strengths in tribal society he gives the weaknesses. We therefore have a true and complete picture in which the whole background is fully realised .... He realistically and convincingly presents many aspects of village life - the feast of the New Yam, the wrestling contest at the *ilo*, the display of the 'egwugwu' on festive occasions, the religious beliefs and activities of the people . . .8

Achebe's descriptions of either the virtues or weaknesses of the society are portrayed by showing how individuals fit within the communal life of the society. It is also through the collective participation of members of the society, in their daily rituals of existence, as noted by Taiwo above, that Achebe creates the impression of "a world". However, it should be noted, as Taiwo says, that Achebe does not judge the issues he presents;[9] rather, he looks "at a situation from very varied points of view, sometimes bringing them before the reader simultaneously. The reader finds, almost invariably, that no one point of view is wholly acceptable and that, to reach a satisfying conclusion, several points of view have to be taken into consideration " (Taiwo, p.112).

Realistic and enlightening as Achebe's portrayal of his society is, his writing is above all else a thematic exploration of the responsibility power imposes on those who exercise it, and of the consequences of its abuse. Achebe creates a cohesive society in *Things Fall Apart,* "with a stable system of values, with precedents of long-standing acceptance, supported by an oral tradition expressed often in proverbial fashion."[10] This is a society that values masculinity, and measures success "in terms of a full barn, a big household of wives and children, a revered position in the councils of elders, titles, and respect due to his position, becomes the factor that defines Okonkwo, gives him respect in the eyes of his clansmen " (Awoonor,p.262). Okonkwo epitomises his society, reflecting as he does its values: "The Igbo, like most African peoples, place great store on the manly virtues as depicted by the wrestling matches and the continous warring between the various clans" (Awoonor, p.252). Achebe's characterisation of Okonkwo accords with

Awoonor's observation; and G. D. Killam puts it most succinctly: "At the centre of the community is Okonkwo, a character of intense individuality, yet one in whom the values most admired by Ibo peoples are consolidated."[11] Illustrating further, and analysing Okonkwo's traits both as an individual, and as an embodiment of the values of his society, Killam says:

> Okonkwo was 'one of the greatest men of his time', the embodiment of Ibo values, the man who better than most symbolized his race ... [and] the premium which is placed on wealth, courage and valour among the Ibo people. Okonkwo was clearly cut out for great things' but he had earned his reputation, as a wrestler (he brought fame to himself and his village); as a warrior (he had taken the approved symbols of his prowess, the heads of five victims by the time he was twenty-one years old); as a man who had achieved personal wealth symbolized by his two barns full of yams, his three wives and, of great importance, the two titles he had taken, titles which can only be acquired when wealth has been achieved and quality proven.
>
> (Killam, p.17)

Eustace Palmer, making basically the same points as Killam, explores the negativism of the society's values:

> Okonkwo is what his society has made him, for his most conspicuous qualities are a response to the demands of his society. If he is plagued by fear of failure and of weakness it is because his society puts such premium on success; if he is obsessed with status it is because his society is preoccupied with rank and prestige; if he is always itching to demonstrate his prowess in war it is because his society reveres bravery and courage, and measures success by the number of human heads a man has won; if he is contemptuous of weaker men it is because his society has conditioned him into despising cowards. Okonkwo is the personification of his society's values, and is determined to succeed in this rat-race.[12]

Critics such as Killam, Palmer, Ravenscroft and Awoonor, among others, all agree that Okonkwo incorporates the virtues of his culture as well as its excesses. Awoonor writes that: "Okonkwo ... embodies all the virtues and excesses of this society. He is a wrestler, a leader, an intrepid farmer, a man of wealth, unyielding in the pursuit of the ways of his fathers .... Around Okonkwo is heard the rhythmic beats of Umuofia's heart" (Awoonor,p.253). But Achebe's characterisation of the society highlights the existence of a balance of values. This is maintained by the integration of the male and aggressive qualities of the society with the female and protective qualities which some of Okonkwo's actions do not reflect. Obierika's counselling and Uchendu's explanation of the philosophy embodied in such a name as 'Nneka' meaning "Mother is supreme" were all attempts to remind Okonkwo of this principle.(*TFA*, p.121). To Okonkwo, the only emotion worth displaying is that of anger, or of a show of strength and manliness, for to him love and affection exemplify weakness. This is the reason for Okonkwo's refusal to believe Obierika's statement that Ogbuefi Ndulue was a strong man in his youth who "led Umuofia to war in those days" (*TFA*, p.62). In Okonkwo's mode of reasoning, a man who "could not do anything without telling" his wife can not be a strong man (*TFA*, p.62). Arthur Ravenscroft notes that "Okonkwo . . . cannot see the wise balance in the tribal arrangement by which the female principle is felt to be simultaneously weak and sustaining."[13] It is on account of Okonkwo's refusal to acknowledge this fundamental concept in his society's world-view that, I believe, he parts ways with his society; and this mostly accounts for his tragedy. Most critics of Achebe's *Things Fall Apart*, particularly Killam, believe that Okonkwo is primarily a victim of the undermining of his culture by the colonisers. However, Achebe's characterisation of Okonkwo indicates that the colonial factor is a catalyst, for Okonkwo's excesses are entirely his own responsibility. As will be seen in the course of this analysis, these excesses are inherent having manifested themselves time and again before he ever comes into contact with any European. For as Ravenscroft notes:

> Achebe implies throughout that Okonkwo is no mere automative victim of a social setting which encourages the qualities he has cultivated. He does have the power of choice; men as highly regarded as he for courage and strength of character are shown not to have expunged gentleness from their hearts. Umuofia may place less value on these gentler virtues but does acknowledge and provide for them.
>
> (Ravenscroft, p.15)

This flexibility of the society contrasts markedly with Okonkwo's single-mindedness, and is most exemplified in the society's legal process. Carroll notes that the judgement scene in *Things Fall Apart* is unique, in that no attempt is made to extract the correct version of the story from the conflicting accounts of the disputants because, "the aim, characteristically, is to balance the disputing claims in order to achieve social justice. . . . By observing the spirit of the law a satisfactory compromise is usually reached which safeguards the solidarity of the group" (Carroll,p.16). Okonkwo, as already mentioned, is shown to symbolise his society's values and exemplifies its virtues, but in Achebe's view he also contrasts with the norms of his society in the degree to which he is inflexible, preferring to apply the letter of the law pertinaciously, rather than to observe its spirit.

Okonkwo's discussion with Obierika after the killing of Ikemefuna highlights this inflexibility. He argues that Ala, the earth goddess could not punish him for obeying her dictates: "The Earth cannot punish me for obeying her messenger . . . . A child's fingers are not scalded by a piece of hot yam which its mother puts into its palm" (*TFA*,p.61). While this argument is sound on a literal level, Ogbuefi Ezeudu's advice to Okonkwo that he should not have a hand in the killing of Ikemefuna because "that boy calls you father", which he ignores shows Okonkwo's lack of appreciation of the cyclical and interweaving nature of the deity's relationship with its worshippers (*TFA*, p.51). Obierika reiterates the same warning when he tells Okonkwo that: "But if the Oracle said that my son should be killed I would neither dispute it nor be the one to do it" (*TFA*, p.61). In Igbo world-view a deity may demand, as Obierika says, that one's child be sacrificed. But unlike the biblical Abraham, the person is neither expected to participate in, nor be the one to do the actual killing. To do either is sacrilegious, *nso ani*, an offence against the earth which was bound to bring retribution on the person from the Earth Goddess despite the argument that the act was committed at the instance of the deity, as Okonkwo reasons. David Carroll's definition aptly describes the role of the Earth Goddess and the deity's relationship with its worshippers:

> Ala, the earth goddess, is usually considered the most powerful [deity]; she is the queen of the underworld and 'owner' of men both dead and alive. Closely associated with the cult of the ancestors, she is also responsible for Igbo morality and her priests provide a powerful integrating force in society by guarding her laws and punishing offenders.

(Carroll, p.17)

However, Achebe indicates how Okonkwo's inherent fear of being like his father, of being thought weak and effeminate, leads him to excesses, even to killing Ikemefuna, who has become like a son to him. Many critics, among them Awoonor, trace Okonkwo's final tragedy to this singular act; an act which Obierika prophetically says is "the kind of action for which the [earth] goddess wipes out whole families" (*TFA,* pp.60-1).

Okonkwo's family is later symbolically wiped out when he commits *nso ani* (crime against the earth) by inadvertently killing a kinsman. But the underlying impetus of Achebe's exploration is the question: To what extent should a man of valour, a man in authority, an elder of the clan, and a possessor of power exercise these? The answer to this question recalls Wole Soyinka's much maligned and often misunderstood comment that a Tiger has no need to proclaim its tigritude; because as Soyinka reasons, when the king of beasts appears it does not need to announce its presence, power, or prowess: it manifests them. All the other animals know this.[14] In Achebe's own words: "You can tell a ripe corn by its look" (*TFA,* p.14).

Okonkwo's fear of being seen to resemble his father, which in turn informs many of his actions, is shown to be unreasonable when Achebe asserts that this society judges a man by his own worth and not that of his father:

> Fortunately, among these people a man was judged according to his worth and not according to the worth of his father . . . Okonkwo . . . had risen so suddenly from great poverty and misfortune to be one of the lords of the clan . . . . But the Ibo people have a proverb that when a man says yes his chi says yes also. Okonkwo said yes very strongly; so his chi agreed. And not only his *chi* but his clan too, because it judged a man by the work of his hands.[15]

Okonkwo has risen from rags and poverty to become one of the lords of the clan, representing his entire village among the assembly of the nine ancestral spirits that symbolise the nine children of the founder of the clan:

> Each of the nine egwugwu represented a village of the clan . . . . The nine villages of Umuofia had grown out of the nine sons of the first father of the clan. Evil Forest represented the village of Umueru, or the children of Eru, who was the eldest of the nine sons . . . . Okonkwo's wives, and perhaps other women as well, might have noticed that the second egwugwu had the springy walk of Okonkwo. And they might also have noticed that Okonkwo was not among the titled men and elders who sat behind the row of egwugwu. . . .The egwugwu with the springy walk was one of the dead fathers of the clan.
>
> (*TFA,* p.81)

At the point at which Achebe opens the narrative Okonkwo has achieved both status and power in the society. What Achebe thus explores is how Okonkwo, having achieved these, uses them. *Things Fall Apart*, being Achebe's first novel and dealing (as it was meant to) with the over-riding theme of showing that Africa had a past and history worthy of note before its first contact with Europe, has this parallel theme of abuse of power, subsumed. But as this analysis will show, it is a theme of which Achebe was conscious even at that early stage in his career as a writer, and which is present in all his writings. This theme is particularly significant to Achebe's exposition of his society's post-colonial tensions. Its germ was sown in *Things Fall Apart* and this is reflected in Achebe's characterisation of Okonkwo and exemplified by what eventually happens to him and the clan.

Achebe writes that Okonkwo was impatient with less successful men: "But he was struck, as most people were, by Okonkwo's brusqueness in dealing with less successful men" (*TFA*, p.24). It is manifest that, having attained a position of success in the society, Okonkwo has forgotten the primal saying that "all fingers are never equal", and that no matter how industrious everyone is, they can never all attain the same measure of success. This insensitivity leads Okonkwo into insulting Osugo, who has taken no title, for contradicting him during a meeting:

> Only a week ago a man had contradicted him at a kindred meeting which they held to discuss the next ancestral feast. Without looking at the man, Okonkwo had said: 'This meeting is for men.' The man who had contradicted him had no titles. That was why he had called him a woman. Okonkwo knew how to kill a man's spirit
> (*TFA*, p.24).

But the ramification of Okonkwo's attitude, his impatience, hot-temper, and brusqueness is more than he even realises, for Achebe says that he was impatient with his father also: "He had no patience with unsuccessful men. He had had no patience with his father" (*TFA*, p.23).

Unoka's fault, Achebe writes, was that he was improvident and a loafer, and not that he was a bad father per se. Achebe mentions that when Okonkwo's crop failed in that terrible year of bad harvest, Unoka, like any father consoled his son, Okonkwo. But even the act of listening to his father was a trying experience for Okonkwo: "Unoka was like that in his last days. His love of talk had grown with age and sickness. It tried

Okonkwo's patience beyond words"(*TFA*, p.23). And as Kofi Awoonor mentions, Okonkwo's response to his father is unnatural and runs contrary to their society's world-view: "This intolerance of failure and contempt for lesser men marks his dealings with his own father, a behaviour which men in Umuofia find unnatural" (Awoonor,p.263). A point which Achebe recalls and reiterates in *No Longer at Ease* with respect to Obi, whose refusal to attend his mother's burial ceremony the people see as an aberration. Given the nature of Umuofia's cultural heritage, a culture where the line of division between the dead, the living, and the unborn is shown to be so thin as to be almost nonexistent, where their symbiotic interaction helps maintain the cosmic cyclical balance of the Igbo world-view, Okonkwo's relationship to his father, which continued even after the man's death, though pragmatic, is nonetheless unwise. In Carroll's definition of the earth goddess (above) he notes that she is "closely associated with the cult of the ancestors" and goes on later to mention that "there is constant interaction between the world of the living and the dead, between the visible and invisible, the material and the spiritual."(Carroll,p.18). Okonkwo's spurning of his father therefore constitutes a break with one of the links that should bind him to the goddess and his other ancestors.

Okonkwo is also shown to be at variance with societal norms in another aspect. Achebe acknowledges that members of Igbo society are traditionally acquisitive and materialistic, but have a spirituality which helps keep the materialism in check:

> Anyone who has given any thought to our society must be concerned by the brazen materialism one sees around. I have heard people blame it on Europe. That is utter rubbish. In fact the Nigerian society I know best - the Ibo society - has always been materialistic. This may sound strange because Ibo life had at the same time a strong spiritual dimension - controlled by gods, ancestors, personal spirits or *chi*, and magic. The success of the culture was the balance between the two, the material and the spiritual.[16]

He goes on further to say: "Today we have kept the materialism and thrown away the spirituality which should keep it in check."[17] Though Okonkwo's "wealth meant the strength of [his] arm" he is however, portrayed as ignoring this spirituality while single-mindedly embracing the materialism.

Added to the above failing, from the traditional society's point of view, Achebe describes Okonkwo's short-temper and heavy-handedness, both with outsiders and with members of his household, as constituting grounds for reproach:

> When he walked, his heels hardly touched the ground and he seemed to walk on springs, as if he was going to pounce on somebody. And he did pounce on people quite often. He had a slight stammer and whenever he was angry and could not get his words out quickly enough, he used his fist . . . . Okonkwo ruled his household with a heavy hand. His wives, especially the youngest, lived in perpetual fear of his fiery temper, and so did his little children.
>
> (*TFA*, pp.4,12)

His inability to control his temper leads him time and again to transgress against the earth goddess, laying a foundation for societal sanction and the explication of the proverb of *nza* the little bird. G.D. Killam has noted that Achebe understates issues, preferring to express more through suggestiveness: "His typical method is based on allusion and implication which leaves much unsaid and thus his writing achieves a suggestiveness which communicates far more than he might achieve in long passages of explicit description"(Killam,p.11). This leads, often, to the apprehension of the symbolic nature of some of Okonkwo's actions, and the society's response to them, only in retrospect.

Achebe characterises Okonkwo as intrepid and aggressive, both in war and on issues of concern to his clan. When one considers this, his high-handedness with members of his immediate family, especially with Nwoye and his younger wives, becomes irrationality bordering on an inability to know when and where to draw the line in exhibiting his manliness. This is most exemplified in his rash reaction to Ekwefi's disparaging remarks about guns that never shot:

> And so when he called Ikemefuna to fetch his gun, the wife who had just been beaten murmured something about guns that never shot. Unfortunately for her, Okonkwo heard it and ran madly into his room for the loaded gun, ran out again and aimed at her as she clambered over the dwarf wall of the barn. He pressed the trigger and there was a loud report accompanied by the wail of his wives and children.
>
> (*TFA*, p.35)

The repercussion to Okonkwo and members of his family would have been very grave had he killed his wife. But most importantly, Achebe suggests that this is an act of irresponsibility. Okonkwo, as a husband, should know and expect that a wife recently chastised or physically brutalised would resort to her most handy weapon - her mouth. He, Achebe believes, should not expect her to extol the praises of her husband under such circumstances, but rather to 'rain' abuses and sarcasm on the husband. Again Okonkwo conveniently forgets the Igbo proverb that "one does not beat a child and forbid the child to cry." Okonkwo's tendency to overreach himself, his inability to control himself and his reaction to events, then, constitute Achebe's charge of abuse of power.

Okonkwo's desecration of the Week of Peace typifies this inability to rein in his temper and his reaction to events. As Achebe notes through Ezeani, the priest of the earth goddess, the forefathers of the clan had ordained that for the good and benefit of the community, no matter what the provocation, no member of the clan should during this week exhibit any manifestation of anger:

> You are not a stranger in Umuofia. You know as well as I do that our forefathers ordained that before we plant any crops in the earth we should observe a week in which a man does not say a harsh word to his neighbour. We live in peace with our fellows to honour our great goddess of the earth without whose blessing our crops will not grow . . . . Your wife was at fault, but even if you came into your obi and found her lover on top of her, you would still have committed a great evil to beat her . . . . The evil you have done can ruin the whole clan. The earth goddess whom you have insulted may refuse to give us her increase, and we shall all perish.
>
> (*TFA*, p.28)

Achebe writes that Okonkwo's other wives in consternation reminded him that it was the sacred week and adds: "But Okonkwo was not the man to stop beating somebody half-way through, not even for fear of a goddess" (*TFA*,p.27). Achebe believes that one of the qualities of a wise person in any society, including the society of *Things Fall Apart,* is for that person to know and acknowledge when he is wrong. This idea is summed up in the Igbo saying that "admitting one's errors is not a mark of cowardice but wisdom." Achebe thus suggests through the comment that Okonkwo was not one to stop anything half-way through, not even when he is in error, that he was not wise. He further states that although inwardly Okonkwo was contrite, "he was not the man to go about telling his neighbours that he was in error" (*TFA*, p.28).

The effect of this stifling of his emotions was that "people said he had no respect for the gods of the clan. His enemies said his good fortune had gone to his head. They called him the little bird *nza* who so far forgot himself after a heavy meal that he challenged his *chi*." (*TFA*,.p.28). Kofi Awoonor establishes the link between Okonkwo's arrogance, his tendency to overreach himself, and his abuse of power and his final tragedy by extending Achebe's imagery of 'the little bird *nza*', and "the great wrestler who, after having defeated all men, went into the spirit world and was confronted with a small wiry spirit who smashed him on the stony earth" (Awoonor,p.267). He further suggests "that perhaps by the very nature of his character, Okonkwo was trying to overreach himself in the public display that accompanies the firing of cannons and guns to salute the dead. So at the height of his achievements and on the verge of achieving greater glories, the gods singled him out for humiliation and destruction" (Awoonor,p.264).

If Awoonor's reading of Okonkwo's tragedy, that he was singled out for destruction by the gods, is correct, Achebe suggests that his fate is consistent with his calling as a warrior, but most especially it reinforces the traditional belief that the tribal gods are efficacious. Achebe believes that the dawn of colonialism rendered Okonkwo's type functionally redundant. It was therefore judicious and necessary that the gods, in performing their traditional function of protecting the clan, and seeing the old warrior who now constituted a time-bomb whose explosion would annihilate the whole clan as exemplified by the story of Abame, should defuse him the way they did. Achebe notes Okonkwo's deviation from the traditional norm of concert, particularly on decisions about whether or not to go to war which would affect the whole clan: "If Umuofia decided to go to war, all would be well. But if they chose to be cowards he would go out and avenge himself .... If they listen to [Egonwanne] I shall leave them and plan my own revenge .... I shall fight alone if I choose" (*TFA*, pp.179-81)

Some critics have noted that Okonkwo commits suicide because he could not face the prospect of seeing the tribe disintegrate under the impact of colonialism, and particularly because he felt that the clan has lost the will to fight like their ancestors: "Okonkwo was deeply grieved. And it was not just a personal grief. He mourned for the clan, which he saw breaking up and falling apart, and he mourned for the warlike men of

Umuofia, who had so unaccountably become soft like women" (*TFA*, p.165). But Achebe sees his tragedy as essentially that of some one whose parochialism blinded him to a complete awareness of the dynamic functioning of his society's response: "Life just has to go on and if you refuse to accept changes, then tragic though it may be, you are swept aside."[18] The society's ability to adapt to any situation, which Carroll has already noted, is a survival mechanism appropriate to the new threat. The clan's action, of choosing not to fight a war they knew they could not win, was consistent with the wisdom of their ancestors contained in the Igbo adage which states that: "The man who cannot discern his superior is immature". Achebe's remark that Okonkwo was swept aside because he refused to accept change accords with the theme of this analysis, that in certain ways he was not representative of his society. While he embodies the acquisitiveness of his society, its materialism, and its love of manliness, Okonkwo persistently shows an aversion to the other 'female' side on which the society's survival depends, and it is this that leads to his tragedy. In Achebe's view, Okonkwo's established deviation from his society, and the fact that most of his excesses were already manifest before he ever comes into contact with any European, indicate abuse of both power and responsibility. These are charges that are even more sustained in *Arrow of God*.

Arrow of God: The Man Behind the Priest - Ezeulu's Usurpation of Ulu's Power and Role

Achebe in an interview with Robert Serumaga in February 1967 says of *Arrow of God* that the society is essentially the same as in *Things Fall Apart:* ."It is the same area - the supporting background and scenery are the same - I'm writing about the same people."[19] But he notes the essential difference between Ezeulu and Okonkwo as being that Ezeulu like the society in this novel, and unlike Okonkwo in *Things Fall Apart*, is "ready to accept change . . . ready to come to terms with it . . . except where his dignity is involved."[20] Killam writes that given the prevailing circumstances at the period, "aware that to resist the white man is impossible and foolhardy, concerned to know as much as he can about the intention of the white man and the nature of his religion and to turn it to his own account, Ezeulu has sent his son Oduche to the mission school" to be his eye there (Killam,p.63). Ezeulu rationalises his action by likening the world to a mask dancing: "If you want to see it well you do not stand in one place. My spirit tells me that those who do not befriend the white man today will be saying *had we known tomorrow*" (*AOG*,pp.45-6). Carroll agrees and says that at the point at which the narrative begins, Europeans had established contact and "the villagers realise they must come to terms with this alien rule which is both powerful and permanent" (Carroll,p.88). As with *Things Fall Apart,* most readings and critics of *Arrow of God* consistently recognise the colonial intervention as a factor in Ezeulu's downfall, even as they acknowledge Ezeulu's tendency, in *Arrow of God*, to mix his wishes with that of his deity. But I believe that Achebe views the colonial intervention as catalytic not causal: "It looked as though the gods and the powers of event finding Winterbottom handy had used him and left him again in order as they found him" (*AOG*, p.230). And as will be evident in the cause of this analysis, Achebe believes Ezeulu, even more than Okonkwo, to be guilty of an abuse of power. Achebe sees the fundamental reasons for his fall as woven into the answer to Ezeulu's own opening analysis of the basis of his power. The colonial factor, in Achebe's view, only accelerated the resolution of the issues which Ezeulu's analysis highlight.

Arrow of God extends the historical perspective found in *Things Fall Apart* and, as in that other novel, Achebe evokes a very realistic world:

> After the priest's familiar world, the most striking feature here, is the externality of the landscape and the climate. As the European records the threat of this alien environment, he makes us realise how convincingly normal is the African world which Achebe has created. There, rituals reflect harmoniously the movement of the seasons as the individual and the environment function together.
>
> (Carroll,p.95)

Arrow of God is also thematically consistent with *Things Fall Apart;* but even more than in that book Achebe's examination of the use and abuse of power is dominant in this novel. While in *Things Fall Apart* this theme was subordinated to that of "putting in a word for [one's] history, . . . tradition,. . . religion, and so on", in *Arrow of God* Achebe culls it out for indepth analysis and, as Carroll says, "chooses for his central character someone who embodies this dilemma in its most acute form -- the chief priest of Ulu" (Carroll,p.91). More than in any other of his writings, it is in this novel that Achebe delineates the relation between the society and their gods, and significantly, what emerges is an illustration of the reciprocity of this relationship. Achebe writes that Ulu was created in response to a special need of the clan:

> In the very distant past . . . the six villages . . . lived as different peoples, and each worshipped its own deity. Then the hired soldiers of Abam used to strike in the dead of night, set fire to the houses and carry men, women and children into slavery. Things were so bad for the six villages that their leaders came together to save themselves. They hired a strong team of medicine-men to install a common deity for them. This deity which the fathers of the six villages made was called Ulu . . . . The six villages then took the name of Umuaro, and the priest of Ulu became their Chief Priest. From that day they were never again beaten by an enemy.
>
> (*AOG*,pp.14-5)

Therefore Ulu's primary purpose and function is the protection of the clan, and as if to underline this utilitarianism Nwaka recounts the experience of a deity in Aninta which failed its society: "And we have all heard how the people of Aninta dealt with their deity when he failed them. Did they not carry him to the boundary between them and their neighbours and set fire on him?"(AOG,p.28).

But between the people and their deity is the priest; whose primary function is to interpret the will of the god to their society. In Nwaka's words, "the man who carries a deity . . . is there to perform [its] ritual and to carry sacrifice to him" (*AOG*, p.27). David Carroll writes:

> Ezeulu's role is to interpret to Umuaro the will of the god and to perform the two most important rituals in the life of the village - the Festival of the Pumpkin Leaves and that of the New Yam. The first of these ceremonies cleanses the six villages of their sins before the planting season . . . .The second . . . sanctifies the harvest and so marks the end of the old year and the beginning of the new.
>
> (Carroll,pp.88-90)

Achebe's exploration exposes not only the dilemma and stresses of a man poised between two worlds, "intermediary between the human world and the spirit world", but those of a man nonetheless who is prone to human foibles (*AOG*, p.89). On this, Achebe, talking to Lewis Nkosi, says: "I'm interested in this old question of who decides what shall be the wish of the gods, and . . . that kind of situation."[21] Achebe's characterisation of Ezeulu assumes importance in the overall quest, particularly because, as I intend to show, Achebe believes that Ezeulu's abuse of the powers vested in him stems from arrogance and total disregard for the ultimate source of his power - the people.

Achebe establishes Ezeulu's arrogance and pride early in the narrative. His philosophical speculations on the nature and scope of his power and relationship to his god and the people only go to underscore this arrogance, pride, and ambition:

> Whenever Ezeulu considered the immensity of his powers over the year and the crops and, therefore, over the people he wondered if it were real. It was true he named the day for the feast of the Pumpkin Leaves and for the New Yam feast; but he did not choose the day. He was merely a watchman. His power was no more than the power of a child over a goat that was said to be his. As long as the goat was alive it was his; he would find it food and take care of it. But the day it was slaughtered he would know who the real owner was. No! the Chief Priest of Ulu was more than that, must be more than that. *If he should refuse to name the day there would be no festival - no planting and no reaping.* But could he refuse? No Chief Priest had ever refused. So it could not be done. He would not dare.(italics mine)
>
> (*AOG*,pp.3-4)

It needs be mentioned at this point that Achebe's characterisation of Ezeulu as one in an intellectual mould ensures that the issue of ignorance becomes untenable, for Ezeulu in his ruminatings would have realised that Ulu, and consequently himself, remain strong and powerful because they are faithful to the original motive and justification for the creation of the god - the protection of the clan; and the clan reciprocates. Achebe in his discussion with Robert Serumaga says of Ezeulu: "He is an intellectual. He thinks about why things happen - of course as a priest; you see, his office requires this - so he goes into things, to the root of things."

In Achebe's view, being the priest of the most powerful deity in a confederation of six villages in a society that traditionally abhors the concentration of too much powers in an individual hand, should have sufficiently alerted Ezeulu to the dangers of even the slightest excesses. Achebe outlines some manifestations of Ezeulu's vanity and pride as prelude to the subsequent happenings: "Ezeulu did not like to think that his sight was no longer as good as it used to be and that some day he would have to rely on someone else's eyes as his grandfather had done when his sight failed . . . . But for the present he was as good as any young man,or better because young men were no longer what they used to be" (*AOG*, p.1). Achebe goes on to show the sort of pranks that he plays on unsuspecting young men: "There was one game Ezeulu never tired of playing on them. Whenever they shook hands with him he tensed his arm and put all his power into the grip, and being unprepared for it they winced and recoiled with pain" (*AOG*, p.1). Achebe sees some element of irresponsibility bordering on juvenility in Ezeulu's act but more than this, it highlights Ezeulu's human side which he seems to acknowledge only when it suits him (I will deal with this later).

Achebe seems to sustain Nwaka's accusations that Ezeulu was ambitious and wanted to arrogate more powers to himself, for he told Bernth Lindfors: "What [Nwaka] was saying in reality was that Ezeulu was getting too powerful . . . . The word 'king' was used here to describe someone who was trying to become too powerful. And this runs against the Ibo belief in the complete integration of life, against their concept of an individual versus society."[22] The concept which Achebe mentions relates to the republican nature of Igbo traditional society, and their recognition of the human tendency to abuse unfettered power.[23] Continuing, Achebe agrees that Ezeulu "had enough priestly arrogance to attempt [to assume too much power]. This shows from time to time, [as] when he is confusing his thinking with the thinking of the god."[24] As Carroll observes, "by means of these two festivals Ezeulu controls both planting and harvesting, and the village year which is dependent upon them", and consequently the people's lives (Carroll,p.91).

The central question which plagues Ezeulu is the extent to which the power he wields is discretionary. This as illustrated in Carroll's analysis emanates from the fact that: "As his ceremonial appearance indicates, Ezeulu is half man, half spirit; in the world of man he is very powerful, in the world of spirits he is a servant" (Carroll,p.91). Ezeulu's dilemma is to find the appropriate position of the individual (himself) in the scheme of things. This also raises two fundamental questions whose resolutions are linked to Ezeulu's final tragedy: "What is the true relationship between the two roles? Where does his primary duty lie, with the god or the tribe?" (Carroll, p.91). Achebe's earlier comment is echoed in Carroll's statement that Ezeulu, "like Okonkwo, ... is convinced that he must obey to the letter the commands of the god; unlike Okonkwo, he alone is equipped to translate these commands to the tribe. In this situation, Ezeulu is constantly tempted to mingle his own wishes with those of the god and then assert his authority over the six villages by means of Ulu's oracular power" (Carroll,pp.91-2). This implies that Ezeulu was aiming at absolute powers which as Achebe mentions is alien to Igbo traditional world-views. In an essay on *chi*, Achebe says:

> At the root of it all lies that very belief ... in the fundamental worth and independence of every man and his right to speak on matters of concern to him and, flowing from it, a rejection of any form of absolutism which might endanger those values. It is not suprisisng that the Igbo held discussion and consensus as the highest ideals of political process. This made them 'argumentative' and difficult to rule. But how could they suspend for the convenience of a ruler limitations which they impose even on their gods.
> (*MYCD*,p.103)

Against this, Ezeulu's rhetorical question to his friend, Akuebue: "Who tells the clan what to say? What does the clan know?" implying as it does that since he knows better than the clan what is best for it, the clan should have taken his advice; assumes significance in contrast (*AOG*,p.131). In Achebe's view, Ezeulu's two roles - as the powerful intermediary for the people and servant of the god - need not be at variance if he adequately recognises his responsibilities and the ultimate source of his power -- for the simple reason that Ulu belongs to, and functions for the benefit of the society. He is therefore both the servant of the god and the people. The inclination of individuals in positions of power to forget the derivative source of their power thus constitutes the main focus of Achebe's enquiry.

To Achebe, the harmonious integration of the traditional society, and the individual's place in that society are reflected in the relationship that exists between the society in its entirety and the deity or deities to which it subscribes. In the Igbo world-view propitiatory rites become essential rituals in the maintenance of this cosmic balance. As Onenyi Nnanyelugo, one of the ten most titled elders and leaders of Umuaro says:

> We have asked Ezeulu what was Ulu's grievance and he has told us. Our concern now should be how to appease him. Let us ask Ezeulu

to go back and tell the deity that we have heard his grievance and we are prepared to make amends. Every offence has its sacrifice, from a few cowries to a cow or a human being.

(*AOG*, pp.208-9).

Ezeulu's response highlights his reluctance to acquiesce in their request: "If you ask me to go back to Ulu I shall do so. But I must warn you that a god who demands the sacrifice of a chick might raise it to a goat if you went to ask a second time." Moreover, such a quibbling response makes his subsequent pronouncements suspect. It is pertinent to recall the argument of Onenyi Nnanyelugo, representing the voice of Umuaro, that the deity would not want Umuaro to perish: "Although I am not the priest of Ulu I can say that the deity does not want Umuaro to perish. We call him the saver." He goes on to spell out Ezeulu's duty and responsibility for him: "Therefore you must find a way out, Ezeulu . . . .It is for you, Ezeulu, to save our harvest." The most important issue in this argument, in Achebe's view, is the fact that, as representatives of Umuaro, the elders and leaders have the inherent right to absolve Ezeulu of any repercussions from the deity for any acts resulting from his obeying their collective wishes:

> Yes, we are Umuaro. Therefore listen to what I am going to say. Umuaro is now asking you to go and eat those remaining yams today and name the day of the next harvest. Do you hear me well? I said go and eat those yams today, not tomorrow; and if Ulu says we have committed an abomination let it be on the heads of the ten of us here. You will be free because we have set you to it, and the person who sets a child to catch a shrew should also find him water to wash the odour from his hand. We shall find you the water.

(*AOG*, p.208)

Achebe deftly structures the complex issue of motive in such a way that, given the society's world-view and the sequence of the events, Ezeulu stands convicted of abuse of power, of arrogating the powers of his deity to himself. As Carroll remarks, "the complexity of [the] opening situation is controlled by the author's narrative focus"; but by the time the different points of view in the argument have been considered, "Ezeulu the man begins to appear from behind the priest" (Carroll, p.94). As has already been mentioned Achebe uses foreshadowing as a structural device. In considering the Umuaro versus Okperi land dispute which is the root of the acrimony in Umuaro (If one excludes the jealousy of the gods and their priests for the moment), the situational ambiguity from which Ezeulu advises the clan has to be put into proper perspective. Of note is that throughout Ezeulu's advice and warnings to the clan, Achebe was careful in his diction; Ezeulu never told the clan that Ulu has categorically forbidden it to go to war because it was a war of blame: "Who would have thought that they would disregard the warning of the priest of Ulu who originally brought the six villages together and made them what they were?" (*AOG*,p.14) As Ezeulu himself suggests: "One half of him was man and the other half *mmo* - the half that was painted over with white chalk at important religious moments. And half of the things he ever did were done by this spirit side" (*AOG*, p.192).

By acknowledging that half of the things Ezeulu ever did were done by his human side, Achebe creates interpretative ambiguity. Later Ezeulu warns: "Is there any man or woman in Umuaro who does not know Ulu, the deity that destroys a man when his life is sweetest to him? . . . . Do [they] think Ulu [will] fight in blame?" (*AOG*, p.27). Again he does not state that Ulu says it will not fight a war of blame. The issue is further compounded by Nwaka's snide but true remark that Ezeulu's mother came from Okperi. Achebe intends the attendant raillery: "One man said that Ezeulu had forgotten whether it was his father or his mother who told him about the farmland" to emphasise the fact that this was a normal village palaver at which every one was entitled to contribute opinion as of right, including Ezeulu (*AOG*, p.16).

Achebe underlines Ezeulu's later reluctance to accede to the wishes of the clan: "Leaders of Umuaro, do not say that I am treating your words with contempt; it is not my wish to do so. But you cannot say: do what is not done and we shall take the blame. I am the Chief Priest of Ulu and what I have told you is his will not mine . . . . The gods sometimes use us as a whip" (*AOG*, p.208). To Ezeulu's argument that they cannot ask him to "do what is not done", a statement which Achebe highlights by italicizing, the elders of the clan replied by giving "numerous examples of customs that had been altered in the past when they began to work hardship on the people" (*AOG*, p.209). This shows that irrespective of what the problem is, its resolution should take account of the general welfare of the clan as its first priority.

Achebe does not only unequivocally indicate Ezeulu's unwillingness to undertake the task of presenting the clan's request to their deity, but when he eventually does accede he is distracted, thus casting doubts on the final result of the quest: "As Ezeulu cast his string of cowries the bell of Oduche's people began to ring. For one brief moment he was distracted by its sad, measured monotone and he thought how strange it was that it should sound so near - much nearer than it did in his compound" (*AOG*, p.210).

If one agrees with such critics as G.D.Killam and Eldred Jones amongst others that the narrative structure of *Arrow of God* is carefully and competently organised, the final resolution of the narrative becomes anticlimactic in that it raises the question of Ezeulu's credibility as a priest. Is he telling the truth when he tells the elders of the clan that the message he has is from Ulu? David Carroll, Kofi Awoonor, G. D. Killam, and even Chinua Achebe all agree that Ezeulu had a tendency to ascribe his wishes to the god, but there is more. This question assumes importance if one recalls that chapter sixteen of the novel ends with the deity, Ulu, mortifying his priest, Ezeulu, for arrogating to himself the powers that rightly belong to his deity, and for plotting revenge, and even scheduling it to suit his convenience: "'Ta! Nwanu!' barked Ulu in his ear, as a spirit would in the ear of an impertinent human child. 'Who told you that this was your own fight?' . . . . 'I say who told you that this was your own fight to arrange the way it suits you? . . . . Beware you do not come between me and my victim or you may receive blows not meant for you!'" (*AOG*, pp.191-2).

But most significant is that Ulu's chastisement comes immediately after Ezeulu has decided what time he plans to have his revenge on Umuaro: "Behind his thinking was of course the knowledge that the fight would not begin until the time of harvest, after three moons more. So there was plenty of time" (*AOG*, p.191). So one would naturally assume that after Ulu's rebuke, Ezeulu would shelve his plans and allow the deity to decide how he wants to conduct the fight, particularly as Ezeulu comments: "It was a fight of the gods. He was no more than an arrow in the bow of his god." But again Achebe foreshadows Ezeulu's later action by adding: "This thought intoxicated Ezeulu like palm wine," an expression which connotes relish. (*AOG*, p.192). If one were to believe, for a moment, that Ezeulu were carrying out the wishes of Ulu, and that he had interpreted Ulu's words as assent for him to punish Umuaro, the above comment dispels that belief. One would think that, in recognition of his role as an intermediary and the portentous implications of the punishment for the clan, "the thought" would not "intoxicate Ezeulu like palm wine".

The opening statement of chapter eighteen plainly demonstrates that Ezeulu's subsequent pronouncements and arguments are suspect. Achebe writes: "After a long period of silent preparation Ezeulu finally revealed [what he had been planning all along] that he intended to hit Umuaro at its most vulnerable point - the Feast of the New Yam" (*AOG*, p.201). There is no indication that this was Ulu's decision. Because Ezeulu's actions are premeditated and calculated to mortally wound, if not destroy the clan, no other resolution of the conflict would have sufficed because as Ezeulu remarks "the punishment was not for now alone but for all time. It would afflict Umuaro like an *ogulu-aro* disease which counts a year and returns to its victim" in order to make the deity impotent, thus destroying the people's dependence on it. Achebe remarks for the second time that:

> So in the end only Umuaro and its leaders saw the final outcome. To them the issue was simple. Their god had taken sides with them against this headstrong and ambitious priest and thus upheld the wisdom of their ancestors - that no man however great was greater than his people; that no one ever won judgement against his clan.
>
> (*AOG*, p.230)

The concluding paragraph is remarkable for its introvertive irony: "If this was so then Ulu had chosen a dangerous time to uphold that truth for in destroying his priest he had also brought disaster on himself." This was precisely the point: that Ulu, by destroying itself, was upholding the basis of its own existence which is to protect the clan. In a world in which it was progressively being made redundant, being likened to a dead god, it was proper that in its death throes the deity should in the face of such unimaginable reccurrent calamity as faced Umuaro raise "to the stature of a ritual of passage" its demise.[25] Obika's death thus becomes an appropriate propitiation in this ritual of passage in conformity with the people's world-view, recalling Onenyi Nnanyelugo's comments about sacrifice of appeasement: "Every offence has its sacrifice, from a few cowries to a cow or a human being." It has to be recalled that at Ulu's creation the clan had sacrificed one of themselves as appropriate to the potency of the "medicine" that became the deity. The god, in reciprocation, efficaciously carried out its functions: "From that day they were never again beaten by an enemy" (*AOG*, p.15).

Faced once more by a threat of similar magnitude, an impending calamity, it is fit that the god should rise to the challenge. But this time the resolution of the foreboding disaster requires the death of the deity itself to avoid the annual reccurence of the problem: "the punishment was . . . for all time. It would afflict Umuaro like an *ogulu-aro* disease which counts a year and returns to its victim." Hence this, as in the creation of the deity, requires a propitiatory sacrifice that is commensurate with the "task" the deity has to perform, of saving the clan. To "cushion" its demise, as in its creation, in accordance with Ibo world-view, requires appropriate sacrifice. Obika's death fulfils this function, but more than this, it represents the most proportional resolution that conclusively incorporates Ezeulu without leaving any loose ends. As in Okonkwo's case, the final resolution has to leave the existence of the society itself uncompromised. Ulu has to vindicate the society's original belief and trust in it, even at the risk of its own destruction, or the downfall of its priest:

> It was not simply the blow of Obika's death, great though it was. Men had taken greater blows: that was what made a man a man. For did they not say that a man is like a funeral ram which must take whatever beating comes to it without opening its mouth; that the silent tremor of pain down its body alone must tell of its suffering?
>
> At any other time Ezeulu would have been a match to his grief. He would have been equal to any pain not compounded with humiliation. But why, he asked himself again and again, why had Ulu chosen to deal thus with him, to strike him down and then cover him with mud?
>
> <div align="right">(<i>AOG</i>, p.229)</div>

In this final resolution, Achebe's repetitive proverb, "that no man however great was greater than his people; that no one ever won judgement against his clan" becomes symbolic. For it evokes and underlines the derivative basis of power which its holders are wont to forget. And in a rhetorical manner becomes the answer to Ezeulu's earlier questioning of the nature of the power and authority which he holds. It also emphasises Achebe's established enquiry, of the responsibility power imposes on those who exercise it, which is taken up in his subsequent writings, particularly his "political" fictions.

CHAPTER THREE

A Legacy Squandered: Achebe's Disillusionment at Post-colonial Irresponsibility in *No Longer at Ease* and *A Man of the People*

No Longer at Ease: The Failure of the First Indigenous Administrative Class

No Longer at Ease is Achebe's second novel, but in the historical time sequence which he has adopted for his works it falls into the third slot after *Things Fall Apart*, which deals with the period, 1850 - 1900,[1] and *Arrow of God*, which deals with the period from 1900 to the late 1920s (Carroll,p.88). *No Longer at Ease* thus brings the period up to approximately 1960. Because of Achebe's conscious use of this time sequence it becomes necessary to disregard the fact that *No Longer at Ease* was published before *Arrow of God*, in order to appreciate not only his development of the themes already identified, but also the progressive sense of disillusionment that pervades both this work and *A Man of the People*.

Achebe's *Things Fall Apart* and *Arrow of God*, while establishing the fact that Africa had a past before its contact with Europe, also show that not all post-colonial tensions have their origin with the colonial encounter. Achebe believes that some of the problems have their roots in pre-colonial society. That these problems arise as a result of some individuals apprehending only partial truths in their society's world-view. In Achebe's view, they have assumed significance and become contemporary problems as a result of society's initial lack of foresight. He believes that the society, in adapting to the 'encounter', failed to be discriminating in its choice of what is necessary from its past for the future: "What values we can take from the past, if we can, as we move along", and what we should not.[2] As Achebe says in the interview with Robert Serumaga:

> But unfortunately when two cultures meet, you would expect, if we were angels shall we say, we could pick out the best in the other and retain the best in our own, and this would be wonderful. But this doesn't happen often. What happens is that some of the worst elements of the old are retained and some of the worst of the new are added on to them.[3]

Achebe illustrates this lack of foresight with some examples, two of which will suffice to exemplify the point. He sees the imported cash economy of Europe as being in consonance with the traditional society's inherent materialistic tendencies. Nevertheless, he says that the post-colonial society's refusal to temper this acquisitive tendency with the traditional spirituality which had hitherto held the materialism in check and maintained a balance, has compounded some of the original problems which the traditional society was able to contain by an adherence to this spirituality. G.D.Killam, talking specifically of *Things Fall Apart,* mentions how the traditional system was upset by the coming of Europeans with their "alien and more powerful system of government, law and Christian religion, coupled with the introduction of a cash economy, the traditional balance between the temporal and spiritual, the male principle of acquisitiveness of which Okonkwo is the archetype, and the female principle of religion embodied in Ani, the Earth Goddess, is upset".[4] Killam's comment ignores the individual's role in maintaining this balance. It ignores the fact that in this society, the balance, welfare, and society's survival, are nurtured by the integration of both the male and female principles, but that the society depends on the individual's appreciation of these for their perpetuation.

Achebe also mentions the inclination of individuals in contemporary society to repudiate traditional values without acquiring adequate substitutes as engendering some of the tensions: "One of the most distressing ills which afflict new nations is a confusion of values".[5] Achebe goes on to describe an incident which he says happened in "1958 or 59":

> There was an accident at a dance in a Nigerian city. Part of the wall collapsed and injured many people -- some seriously. Incredible as it may sound, some car-owners at the dance refused to use their cars to convey the injured to hospital. One man was reported as saying that his seatcovers would be ruined . . . . It merely shows a man who has lost one set of values and has not yet acquired a new one -- or rather has acquired a perverted set of values in which seatcovers come before a suffering human being. I make bold to say that such an incident could not have happened in a well-knit traditional African society.[6]

Achebe sees this clash of values or more appropriately, lack of values in the post-colonial society as one of the principal causes of the post-colonial tensions in the society. Obi Okonkwo, the protagonist, of Achebe's *No Longer at Ease* illustrates this modern phenomenon as this analysis will prove. But more important in Achebe's view, is the fact that at the period just before independence the destiny of many of the new nations of Africa were in the hands of the emergent black administrative class, represented by Obi Okonkwo. In this class were vested the authority and privilege of shaping and mapping out the course that these colonies would take on independence, and of laying the foundations on which democracy could be built. Neal Ascherson, remarking of the hope placed on Obi's generation, states: "In this decade of African catastrophe, it is hard to reconstruct the optimism and certainties of the emergent African political class thirty years ago, and of their liberal-minded European sympathizers. Independence seemed the happy-ever-after conclusion. . . ."[7]

It is necessary from the outset to establish that Obi Okonkwo is a representative character and that Achebe uses him to illustrate the dilemma of the society at large, and of "the Nigeria" in a state of flux: "Obi Okonkwo is a representative of the African intelligentsia which, on the eve of independence, looked upon itself - and was looked upon by ex-colonial powers, as well as by the masses of Africa - as the natural leaders of the new society."[8] They were thus accorded all the privileges, and given all the authority necessary to accomplish this task for the future of their people. The society, in Achebe's view, had also gone to an extraordinary length to "create", equip, and set this class apart, as its future leaders through education:

> Six or seven years ago Umuofians abroad had formed their union with the aim of collecting money to send some of their brighter young men to study in England. . . .They had taxed themselves mercilessly to raise eight hundred pounds to send him [Obi] to England. Some of them earned no more than five pounds a month. . . .They had wives and school-going children.
>
> (*NLE*, pp.7,98).

Achebe further states that the society had "laboured in sweat and tears to enrol Obi", and by extension his class, "among the shining élite" (*NLE*,p.98).

But the society had done these things, creating and educating the "Obis", with specific expectations. In the traditional society, one's first responsibility is the recognition that within the framework of that culture from which the individual sprang, the person's duty, as defined by David Carroll, "is the constant awareness of the self as an integral part of the organic whole of the village or tribe through which one acts or achieves identity" (Carroll,p.78) The society, in recognition of the above, trained this class of people in the belief that whatever skills they acquire would be used for the benefit of the society. Achebe's *No Longer at Ease*, therefore, explores how this class discharged their mandate, and what the consequences have been for society of their failure to discharge this obligation honourably.

Achebe, at the time of writing *No Longer at Ease*, was concerned that, as heirs of the new order, this new emergent black administrative class might not have been adequately equipped for the task of self governance (since it is assumed that democratic processes demand very high standards of commit-

ment, honesty and, above all, responsibility in those vested with authority, to be productive, meaningful and sustained). Mr Green tells Obi :
> You know, Okonkwo, I have lived in your country for fifteen years and yet I cannot begin to understand the mentality of the so-called educated Nigerian. Like this young man at the University College, for instance, who expects the government not only to pay his fees and fantastic allowances and find him an easy, comfortable job at the end of his course, but also to pay his intended [fiancee]. It's absolutely incredible. I think Government is making a terrible mistake in making it so easy for people like that to have so-called University Education. Education for what? To get as much as they can for themselves and their family. Not the least bit interested in the milllions of their country-men who die everyday from hunger and disease.
> (*NLE*, p.116)

Granted, Mr Green, as John Povey says, "is not an agreeable man to represent a moral stand point",[9] but despite his sarcastic tone, or even because of it, Achebe uses him to point at underlying problems of both the emergent black administrative class represented by Obi, and to Nigeria as a country in transition: "There is no single Nigerian who is prepared to forgo a little privilege in the interest of his country. From your Ministers down to your most junior clerk. And you tell me you want to govern yourselves" (*NLE*, p.153). Considering the social circumstances of the period, that this was a society in transition, Achebe believes that Obi and his class were symbolic pioneers. The philosophy espoused by the President of Umuofia Progressive Union shows what the society expects of its pioneer class: "We are pioneers building up our families and our town. And those who build must deny ourselves many pleasures" (*NLE*, p.82).

Ironically, the antagonism of Obi Okonkwo for "the Greens" and the stereotypical picture of Mr Green, dims the poignacy of his message -"that a country that is born on a cesspool of bribery and corruption" was not mature enough to value democracy.[10] I should hasten to say that the Nigeria of *No Longer at Ease*, on the verge of transiting from a colony into an independent nation, is not unlike a villager from a rural community in his first journey to an urban environment. Both demand tentative, almost hesitant steps and constant vigilance, or else, just as the villager is liable to be run-over by a moving vehicle in the unaccustomed bustle of the city if he is not careful, or miss his way, the country is also liable to collapse or be destroyed, if those vested with authority are not honest, responsible, and careful.

It is my contention that Achebe portrays this Nigeria in terms that are similar to the way he portrays the main character, Obi Okonkwo. The problems that beset both are similar, and their solutions or lack of solutions are also similar. Achebe's analysis of the problems and challenges that this emergent black administrative class, which Obi represents, face as a result of both societal and family demands and expectations, and how they respond to these, shows why he indicts them of irresponsibility.

It is through the effective use of flashback, that Achebe attempts to explore the various factors that are responsible for the failure of Obi and his class. The satirical ending Achebe gives *No Longer at Ease*, which is also the beginning of the narrative, begins this exposition:

> Everybody wondered why. The learned judge, as we have seen, could not comprehend how an educated young man and so on and so forth. The British council man, even the men of Umuofia did not know. And we must presume that in spite of his certitude, Mr Green did not know either".
>
> (*NLE*,p.170)

By beginning the narrative at the end, and doubling back, Achebe traces "where the rain began to beat the society".

Achebe believes that members of this class did not seem to comprehend the enormity of the responsibility asked of them as representatives of the people at large. They are depicted as having adopted the common attitude which sees the government as an amorphous, unquantified establishment to which they owe no personal commitment: "'Have they given you a job yet?' the Chairman asked Obi over the music. In Nigeria the government was 'they'. It had nothing to do with you or me. It was an alien institution and people's business was to get as much from it as they could without getting into trouble" (*NLE*, p.33).

Even the education which the society makes possible for this class, becomes for them, a means to material acquisition:

> A University degree was the philosopher's stone. It transmuted a third-class clerk on one hundred and fifty a year into a senior Civil Servant on five hundred and seventy, with car and luxuriously furnished quarters at nominal rent. And the disparity in salary and amenities did not tell even half the story. To occupy a 'European post' was second only to actually being a European. It raised a man from the masses to the elite whose small talk at cocktail parties was: "How's the car behaving?"
>
> (*NLE*, p.92)

As Mr Green remarks, education, to Obi and his class, is a means "to get as much as they can for themselves and their family." None of them is shown to be "the least bit interested in the millions of their country-men who die everyday from hunger and disease." Neither were they prepared, as Mr Green also says, "to forgo a little privilege in the interest of [their society]".

Achebe views maturing for an individual as having a lot in common with a country on the verge of attaining independence, both demand more than the average sense of responsibility. Obi and his class are shown to be interested only in the material perquisites of their positions: "Obi bought a Morris Oxford a week after he received his letter of appointment. Mr Green gave him a letter to the dealers saying that he was a senior civil servant entitled to a car advance. *Nothing more was required. He walked into the shop and got a brand-new car*" (*NLE*,p.66 italics mine). Earlier in the day Obi had been given sixty pounds as 'outfit" allowance. "'You think Government give you sixty pounds without signing agreement?' It was only then that Obi understood what it was all about. He was to receive sixty pounds outfit allowance" (*NLE*,p.67). Even this early in Obi's career, he is shown to embody the perverse corruption which he criticises, as he falsifies his statement of expenditure after receiving another allowance because he "had not realised that the allowance was not a free gift to be spent as one liked"

The scramble, for Obi and his class, is for the distribution of what Nigerians call "the national cake" This metaphor likens the economic resources of the nation to a cake which exists so that anyone in a position to do so, might carve from it as big a piece as he possibly can for himself and his family and, by extension, for his tribe or ethnic group.

Achebe thus identifies Nigeria's tragedy as the fact that the country, even at birth, already carried the germs of decay, through the still-born idealism of such people as Obi Okonkwo. As Gerald Moore notes: "Achebe does not see Obi Okonkwo as a tragic hero. The pressures that pull and mould him are all pressures making for compromise and accommodation . . . . But Obi is destroyed by 'doing what everyone does;' by running away from scandal, living above his income, taking bribes" (Moore,pp.70-1).

The economic and materialistic tensions that Obi Okonkwo experiences in *No Longer at Ease* need be put into perspective to explain why Achebe is preoccupied with the notion of 'responsibility'. It is my view that to Achebe, the term "responsibility" is central to the resolutions or understanding of the tensions and problems of Obi Okonkwo, the Nigerian elite class he represents, and the Nigerian state.

If we organise the "evidence" which Achebe presents to us, and if we treat Obi as a real person, as Achebe's kind of social realism invites us to do, then we find that a lot of Achebe's criticisms and his stern reproof of this class begin to make sense. Obi is on a salary of forty-seven pounds and ten shillings (£47.10). Tabulated below are the economic demands on him both obligatory and self imposed:

	Annual			Monthly		
	£	s	d	£	s	d
Insurance	42 .	-		3	10	-
John's School fees	49.	10	-	4	2	-
Income Tax	32 .			2	13	4
His parents	120 .	-		10	-	
Repayments to U.P.U	240 ..	-		20	-	
Driver's salary	54 ..	-		4	10	-
Electricity bills	64	7	-	5	7	3

Steward's salary*	42	-	-	3	10	-
Gardener's salary	6	6	-	-	10	6
Fuel and vehicle maintainance	60	-	-	5	-	-
Feeding and entertainment	120			10	-	
Incidental expenses	60	-	-	-	5	-
Total	890	3	--	74	3	1[11]

Achebe, foreshadowing Obi's financial irresponsibility, had said through Mr Green, "You will do well to remember . . . that at this time every year you will be called upon to cough up forty pounds for insurance. . . . It is, of course, none of my business really. But in a country where even the educated have not reached the level of thinking about tomorrow, one has a clear duty"(*NLE*,p.95). When the insurance letter came, Obi "had just a little over thirteen pounds in the bank", thus proving Mr Green's assessment of him, and the class he represents, to be correct. For a civil servant who has no other source of income, but his monthly salary of forty-seven pounds and ten shillings (£47.10), to be spending about seventy-four pounds, three shillings and seven pence indicated financial imprudence and lack of planning and foresight - or an anticipation of illegal means of getting the difference.

Considering the earlier remark about the society's expectations from its class of pioneers, it is enlightening at this point to analyse Obi's expenses with a view to determining which of them are not really important or necessary. This exercise will also be helpful in ascertaining Achebe's views about the main character and his role. The first thing to note is that Obi's pride and his refusal to accept the four months period of grace before starting the repayment of the loan for his studies, put pressure on his finances and compounded his lack of planning (which I will come to later):

> Take this matter of twenty pounds every month to his town union, which in the final analysis was the root of all his troubles. Why had he not swallowed his pride and accepted the four months' exemption which had been allowed, albeit with bad grace? Could a person in his position afford that kind of pride? Was it not a common saying among his people that a man should not, out of pride and etiquette, swallow his phlegm?
>
> <div align="right">(<i>NLE</i>,pp.155-6)</div>

Obi did not need a driver and could have saved himself the monthly payment of four pounds and ten shillings (£4.10), but in keeping with the status of a "senior service" and to boost his ego, he hired one. Also with his deep involvement with Clara, and by the steward's admission that Clara still cooks for Obi, his need for a steward was minimal. Achebe indicates this through Sebastin's statement that: "God knows Clara used twice as much meat when she made the soup herself!" and so Obi could have dispensed with the services of a steward. This could have saved him not only the salary, but another mouth to feed and thus also reduce his monthly feeding expenses. Since Clara's feeding in Obi's house cannot be quantified because she has her own house and Obi, we will assume, also eats at her house when he visits her, one will base the analysis on the fact that only two people live in Obi's house - Obi himself and the steward. Therefore, dispensing with the steward would reduce the feeding expenses by almost fifty per cent (although there are other variables that one should not go into here for the sake of simplicity). Doing away with the services of the steward would also reduce the consumption of electricity because the steward's quarters would then not use as much power as when occupied, plus the other sundry expenses and electricity consumptions which Obi pays for by virtue of the steward's presence in the house.

So merely dispensing with the duties of the driver and the steward would have reduced Obi's expenses by as much as fifteen pounds a month both in wages, feeding, and lighting. Thus, with the other adjustments that any responsible man "starting life" has to make in his day to day existence, like not being pig-headed, swallowing his pride when it is necessary, budgeting his expenses against his income and avoiding such extravagance as buying an engagement ring worth twenty pounds (£20.00) at a period when one shilling could buy fifty cups of garri,[12] Obi could have lived within his means.

Having looked at the financial demands on Obi Okonkwo, it is necessary to also assess the societal expectations and demands on him. This is important as both demands cannot really be divorced from each other. Society expects Obi and his class to reflect their pioneer status in their behaviour. Paradoxically, the same society expects them to live like elites, with all the trappings that the type of life demand - a car, driver, steward and other such luxuries:

> What they did not know was that, having laboured in sweat and tears to enrol their kinsman among the shining elite, they had to keep him there. Having made him a member of an exclusive club whose members greet one another with 'How's the car behaving?' Did they expect him to turn round and answer: 'I'm sorry, but my car is off the road. You see I couldn't pay my insurance premium.' That would be letting the side down in a way that was quite unthinkable. Almost as unthinkable as a masked spirit in the old Ibo society answering another's esoteric salutation: 'I'm sorry, my friend but I don't understand your strange language. I'm but a human being wearing a mask.' No, these things could not be.
>
> (*NLE*, p.98)

The society also expects that they use their positions to the benefit of their own people. Umuofia Progressive Union's discussion on Joshua's plight, reflects this:

> Joshua is now without a job. We have given him ten pounds. But ten pounds does not talk. If you stand a hundred pounds here where I stand now, it will not talk. That is why we say that he who has people is richer than he who has money. Everyone of us here should look out for openings in his department and put in a word for Joshua . . . . Thanks to the Man Above,' he continued, 'we now have one of our sons in the senior service. We are not going to ask him to bring his salary to share among us. It is in little things like this that he can help us. It is our fault if we do not approach him. Shall we kill a snake and carry it in our hands when we have a bag for putting long things in?'
>
> (*NLE*, pp.79-80)

The society, represented in this instance by Umuofia Progressive Union, expects Obi to use his position to the advantage of the immediate family represented also in this context by the people of the same tribe or kindreds - to find jobs for his people irrespective of whether the applicants are qualified for the jobs or not. No one questions the morality of the expectations. The prevailing feeling is that as long as he is doing it for "us" it is all right, "us" referring to people from his tribe, clan, or kindred.

Obi is also expected to look sophisticated, dress in European suits and speak like a "been to":[13]

> Everybody was properly dressed in agbada or European suit except the guest of honour, who appeared in his shirt sleeves because of the heat. That was Obi's mistake Number One. Everybody expected a young man from England to be impressively turned out .... Obi's English on the other hand, was most unimpressive. He spoke 'is' and 'was' .... when he sat down the audience clapped from politeness. Mistake Number Two.
>
> *(NLE, pp.31-3)*

While expecting him to be sophisticated, dress and generally behave like a "been to", the society also believes and expects Obi to maintain his links with the tradition and culture of his people. More than anything, it is this antinomy that Obi finds hardest to reconcile. The vehemence with which his association with Clara - an *osu* - is received by everyone clearly exemplifies this duality.

At this point it becomes necessary to define what an *osu* is in order that Obi's predicament may be more easily appreciated. An *osu* in Igboland is a person, male or female, who is dedicated to any of the gods or goddesses. The person's origin is immaterial. He or she becomes the property of the god or goddess and may not marry or be married by any person other than another *osu*.. Because they are taboo, even their intercourse with the freeborn are very limited, and it was not until the advent of christianity into Igboland that it became possible for an *osu* and a freeborn to sit under the same roof. The traditional sanction on the *osu* system is so powerful that to this day, in some areas of Igboland, any freeborn who marries an *osu* automatically becomes an outcast or *osu* and their offspring forever become outcasts.

When Joseph heard that Obi intends to marry an *osu*, his reaction typified the traditional reaction to such a "preposterous" idea: "'You know book, but this is no matter for book. Do you know what an osu is? But how can you know?' In that short question he said in effect that Obi's mission house upbringing and European education had made him a stranger in his country - the most painful thing one could say to Obi."

The President of Umuofia Progressive Union in his own reaction says: "You may ask why I am saying all this. I have heard that you are moving with a girl of doubtful ancestry, and even thinking of marrying her . . ." and that is as far as he gets before Obi's rage erupts and he stumps out of the meeting. Christopher who is the only character in the book most likely to understand Obi's predicament and appreciate his point of view is even more dogmatic: "You may say that I am not broad-minded, but I don't think we have reached the stage where we can ignore all our customs. You may talk about education and so on but I am not going to marry an *osu*" (*NLE*, p.144).

Obi's father's reaction is even more graphic. On learning the name of Clara's father, he laughed. Achebe writes that: "It was the kind of laughter one sometimes heard from a masked ancestral spirit . . . . And the meaning of that laughter was clear: 'I did not really think you would know; you miserable human worm!'"(*NLE*, p 132). When Obi uses the biblical arguments that "we are Christians", and that "the Bible says that in Christ there are no bond or free", he only elicits a pause and a sombre reply from his father. Obi's father goes on to explain:

> 'My son, . . . I understand what you said. But this thing is deeper than you think . . . . I know Josiah Okeke very well . . . . I know him and I know his wife. He is a good man and a great Christian. But he is Osu. Naaman, the captain of the host of Syria, was a great man and honourable, he was also a mighty man of valour, but he was a leper.'
>
> '. . . . Osu is like leprosy in the minds of our people. I beg of you, my son, not to bring the mark of shame and of leprosy into your family. If you do, your children and your children's children unto

the third and fourth generations will curse your memory . . . . You will bring sorrow on your head and on the heads of your children. Who will marry your daughters? Whose daughters will your sons marry? Think of that, my son. We are Christians, but we cannot marry our own daughters.'

(*NLE*,pp.133-4)

Isaac Okonkwo thus sums up the society's attitude to the *osu* and more importantly shows that the problem transcends the immediate. If Obi marries Clara, their offspring become outcasts and subject to societal discrimination for ever. Obi's dilemma is that his Christian upbringing, western education, and his own emotions have not adequately prepared him for these antinomies - demanding that he be sophisticated and urbane while at the same time retaining and espousing the tradition and culture of his people, even when these traditions and cultures run counter to his own wishes and principles.

Having said all this, one questions why Achebe should choose for his hero, a man who is naive enough to leave the sum of fifty pounds (£50.00) which he borrowed, in the glove compartment of his car while going into a night club, particularly at a time when he is in a financial crisis, and a man who does not know that a worker who earns income has to pay income tax? The answers to these questions are interwoven with Achebe's belief that Obi and his class lacked any sense of both individual and collective responsibilities. Achebe in an analysis of what he believes is the trouble with Nigeria, in a booklet, *The Trouble with Nigeria*, writes that: "The Nigerian problem is the unwillingness or inability of its leaders to rise to the responsibility, to the challenge of personal example which are the hallmarks of true leadership."[14] Achebe also questions, through Mr Green, whether Obi and his class actually appreciate the "responsibility" that is demanded of them by the very act of setting them apart. He consistently contrasts Mr Green's attitude to duty with Obi's to expose the difference between one attitude that is responsible and another one that is not. It is of note that Mr Green tendered his resignation when he felt that the country was going to be granted independence in 1956: "they said he had put in his resignation when it was thought that Nigeria might become independent in 1956. In the event it did not happen and Mr Green was persuaded to withdraw his resignation" (*NLE*, p.105).

In Mr Green, Achebe has painstakingly portrayed a man of unquestionable integrity, devoted to his duties and very responsible. As Obi himself agrees:

> Take, for instance, his devotion to duty. Rain or shine, he was in the office half an hour before the official time, and quite often worked long after two, or returned again in the evening. Obi could not understand it. Here was a man who did not believe in a country, and yet worked so hard for it. Did he simply believe in duty as a logical necessity? He continually put off going to see his dentist because, as he always said, he had some urgent work to do
>
> (*NLE*, p.105)

It is evident from the above, and the comments of Miss Tomlinson that "he pays school fees for his steward's sons," coupled with the fact that all his comments about the emergent administrative class - the educated Africans - are true; that Achebe has sympathies for Mr Green's point of view. For Mr Green, it is not just a question of not believing in the country as Obi says, but not believing in the administrative capabilities of the new emergent black administrative class which Obi represents. Miss Tomlinson comments that Mr Green "says the most outrageous things about educated Africans", and as Achebe indicates, all his comments about educated Africans "not being capable of handling their own affairs", in respect of Obi, prove to be true.[15] It is no wonder then that a man as dedicated to building the country as he is, humane to his employees, understandably could not bear to see his years of hardwork dissipated by the naivety and incompetence of administrators like Obi Okonkwo:

> Charles - you know the messenger - told me that sometime ago the A.A. wanted to sack him for sleeping in the office. But when the matter went up to Mr Green, he tore out the query from Charles's personal file. He said the poor man must be suffering from malaria, and the next day he bought him a tube of quinacrine.
>
> (*NLE*, pp.104-5)

Achebe sees Obi's argument, that the black emergent administrative class learnt their corrupt attitudes from their colonial masters, as balderdash: "It is not the fault of Nigerians . . . . You devised these soft conditions for yourselves when every European was automatically in the senior service and every African automatically in the junior service. Now that a few of us have been admitted into senior service, you turn around and blame us"(*NLE*, p.154). Obi's comments about Mr Green's dedication to service, cited earlier, proves this assertion wrong. When one compares Obi's frequent leaves of absence with Miss Tomlinson's remarks that Mr Green even defers seeing his dentist because of his commitment to duty, it becomes obvious that Achebe also does not agree with Obi's above assertion. Miss Tomlinson states that: "'There's a lot of truth in what he [Mr Green] says,'. . . . 'I'm sure there is.' 'I don't mean about you, or anything of the sort. But quite frankly, there are too many holidays here. Mark you, I don't really mind. But in England I never got more than two weeks' leave in the year. But here, what is it? Four months '"(*NLE,* pp.153-4).

Even if Obi's statement were true, there is an Igbo adage that "a man does not toss his loin-cloth into the fire because he sees those of his relations in flames." This implies that even if the colonial administrators were corrupt, the emergent black administrators as "sons of the soil" need not have followed suit, were they truly responsible and committed to building up their country. Instead, they destroy what "the Greens" have already built.

Obi and his class have, by virtue of academic attainment, been admitted into the privileged circle of leaders without having acquired the intrinsic qualities that go with it. They have in the course of gaining western type education (which calls for a whole new way of evaluating issues) lost or discarded their traditional values. But in acquiring the academic knowledge, they have not acquired those intrinsic cultural qualities which only long-term socialization in the culture can give. As Carroll notes, talking of Christian converts and educated Africans:

> Converts were not simply substituting a Christian for a tribal god; they were exchanging a religion through which they were identified

with the tribe for a religion without any such affiliations. This is
why the security and power offered by the impressive missionary
educational system were so necessary. The converts for a variety of
reasons had jettisoned the rationale of traditional African life, and
now they were to be given a vital role in the new forms of society
which the missionaries were creating out of the destruction of the
old. These forms, it should be added, were often opposed to those
predictable structures legislated by the administrators.

(Carroll, pp.9-10)

But Achebe sees a fundamental flaw in the whole equation as being that certain values (some already mentioned) can only be internalised through thorough socialisation. This could not be acquired with a three or four years stint abroad. Achebe, I believe, is concerned that with products like Obi at the helm of affairs, Nigeria was not adequately prepared for the responsibility of being independent. Achebe's problem was that to openly assert that this was the case would have turned the ire of the people against him, particularly at a time that people were clamouring for independence. Odili nevertheless makes the point in *A Man of the People* : "Poor black mother! Waiting so long for her infant son to come of age and comfort her and repay her for the years of shame and neglect. And the son she has pinned so much hope on turning out to be a Chief Nanga. . . . It is a favourite of my father's who, by the way, still thinks we should never have asked the white man to go"(*AMOP*, pp.91-2). And also the Minister, Hon. Sam Okoli in *No Longer at Ease*: "'Whiteman don go far. We just dey shout for nothing' . . . . Then he seemed to realise his position. 'All the same they must go. This no be them country'"(*NLE*, p.68). Hon. Sam Okoli concluded by saying that ". . . our people have a long way to go " (*NLE,* p.69).

Achebe is particularly disgusted with the institutionalisation of corruption as a way of life by the high and low of the country. He painstakingly documents the views of people from all walks of life on bribery, because it is an issue that he sees as central to the whole concept of responsibility. Achebe is of the view that the corruption of illiterate officials while inexcusable could be understood within the context of Obi's analysis: "But take one of these old men he probably left school thirty years ago in Standard Six. He has worked steadily to the top through bribery - an ordeal by bribery. To him the bribe is natural. He gave it and expects it. Our people say that if you pay homage to the man on top, others will pay homage to you when it is your turn to be on top"(*NLE*, p.21).

But Obi and his class as pioneers, their job was to liberate the society from such social injustices inherited from the ancients as the caste system. They were to map out the direction for the future of the society by dismantling such structures that necessitate an "ordeal by bribery". Most especially, having been to "the mother country", and having witnessed democracy in practice, and all that sustains and buttresses it, Obi and his class are expected to "show" their people the light. They are expected to lay the precedents by which the society would function, evaluate, and judge the actions of their leaders. This is particularly important since the checks and balances which functioned well in the traditional system, were now powerless in the new dispensation.

But the perpetuation of the status quo which Obi's succumbing to corruption implies represents a negation of this hope. It also suggests that the minister, and the class that Obi referred to in his analysis of "ordeal by bribery", would continue to flourish. The Igbo have an adage which states that "it is when people are drunk that they lose all inhibitions and reveal their real and innermost thoughts." The Minister in "his unguarded moment" had actually revealed a view held by most people in the country, that there is nothing wrong with giving and receiving bribes. One of the members of the panel that interviewed Obi when he applied for job, as if to confirm that bribery had been ordained, asked Obi: "Why do you want a job in the civil service? So that you can take bribes?"(*N L E*, p.40). It is pertinent to remember that this statement or question is the man's only contribution throughout the lengthy interview.

To Achebe, the most repulsive thing about bribery is not the custom officer's open extortion: "I can be able to reduce it to two pounds for you . . . .I fit do it, but you no go get Government receipt "(*NLE*, p.30). It is not even the policemen's history of demanding bribes on the highways: '"How much they take?" asked the driver."Ten shillings" gasped his assistant '(*N L E*, p.43). It is the general apathy of the people to corruption.

Obi is generally blamed either for taking a paltry sum:". . . the president said it was a thing of shame for a man in the senior service to go to prison for twenty pounds. He repeated "twenty pounds", spitting it out. 'I am against people reaping where they have not sown. But we have a saying that if you want to eat a toad you should look for a fat and juicy one'" (*NLE*, p.6). Or, blamed for being naive in the art of taking bribes: "It is all lack of experience . . . . He should not have accepted the money himself. What others do is tell you to go and hand it to their houseboy" (*NLE*, p.6). Obi is never blamed for the corrupt practice itself. To the people, Obi's sin is not in being corrupt, but inept.

It is true that there are societal demands on Obi and his class. For, Achebe does not underrate the difficulty of the task that Obi and his class are called upon to perform. Some of these demands are apparently conflicting, but Achebe questions if the tensions such demands generate are too much for Obi and this class to contain. As has been mentioned, Achebe considers the issue of both personal and collective "responsibility" as central to the whole concept of self-governance, and he sees Obi Okonkwo as typical of the average Nigerian graduate of the period who were the inheritors of the new nation. . . .As has also been illustrated, society expects Obi, by virtue of his position, to demand and accept bribes as his due. As Joseph's friend tells him in respect of Obi: '"E go make plenty money there. Every student who wan' go England go de see am for house. "E no be like dat," said Joseph. "Him na gentleman. No fit take bribe." "Na so," said the other in unbelief' (*NLE*, p.77). The society also expects those who indulge in such dishonest activities, as Obi does, to be clever enough not to be caught: "Obi tried to do what every— one does without finding out how it was done" (*NLE*, p.6). Paradoxically the same society, as exemplified by Joseph's implicit defence of Obi, believes that he [Obi] and his class should be gentlemen of honour, and that they should refuse such corruptive influences, and thus usher in a new era. It is therefore these contradictions, and Achebe's comments about no one understanding why Obi succumbs to corruption, that *No Longer at Ease* tries to explicate.

Achebe sees the resolution of these conflicting demands as only possible through the actions of people who are exposed to both worlds, as Obi and his class are. As already indicated, Achebe like Ihimaera, sees the ideal solution to the post-colonial tensions as being the merger of the positive values of both cultures -- European and indigenous -- but this, he says, is not always possible. Achebe believes that it is only Obi and his class, by virtue of their exposure to both cultures that could begin to even contemplate this merger. Obi and his class thus represented, for the society, this hope. They also embodied the society's main hope of being liberated from both old dogmas and the shackles of established corruption. For, as Achebe explains, only those with a "proper sense of history" and a vision of where their society should be heading, could help their society.

Unfortunately, Achebe characterises Obi as both naive and having no proper sense of history. He achieves the first by exposing the superficiality of Obi's responses in his dealings and relationships with other characters, particularly with Clara and with Umuofia Progressive Union. As Cook says: "In all these delicate relationships Obi contrasts unfavourably with the elders of the Union."[16] Achebe achieves the second through glimpses of Obi's past, and his alienation from his people, and from his roots.

Obi's alienation stems both from his upbringing and his liberal western education. Traditionally, a child in Igboland belongs to the community and his obeisance to the culture and tradition of his people rests as much on what the child picks up instictively by association with other children and the community at large, as on the parent's teachings. By depriving Obi of this second and fundamental part of his 'childhood lessons,' his parents had helped alienate him from his roots:

> Isaac Okonkwo was not merely a Christian; he was a catechist. In their first years of married life he made Hannah see the grave responsibility she carried as a catechist's wife. And as soon as she knew what was expected of her she did it, sometimes showing more zeal than even her husband. She taught her children not to accept food in neighbours' houses because she said they offered their food to idols. That fact alone set her children apart from all others, among the Ibo, children were free to eat where they liked.
>
> (*NLE*,p.58)

This childhood upbringing has not only enstranged Obi from his culture, it has also made him ignorant of his responsibility to the community. Recalling Carroll's comment on the place of the individual within the traditional society, and Cook's similar views, Obi exhibits a marked ignorance of his society's worldview. This ignorance is further compounded by his sense of individualism resulting from his western education.

The society had trained Obi with the expectations that he would return to them "with the boon of prophetic vision".[17] But Obi returns with an acquired and heightened sense of his individuality, plus an inclination to benefit from the traditional communal sense of solidarity and kinship. Obi seeks the benefit of the communal solidarity which made his education possible along with the liberal notion of individuality which has no place in the traditional society. In his address to the Lagos branch of Umuofia Progressive Union, Obi had said that: "Our fathers also have a saying about the danger of living apart. They say it is the curse of the snake. If all snakes lived together in one place, who would approach them? But they live every one unto himself and so fall prey to man"(*NLE*, p.81). It is evident that Obi cannot have the best of both worlds. His insubordination to Umuofia Progressive Union is only an expression of the desire to be his own man, but viewed from the cultural perspective, Obi is seen as an ingrate. Obi's inability to appreciate the role of elders in the Igbo world view as aptly described by Adrian Roscoe testifies to his alienation:

> In the society that Achebe's novels often portrays, it is the tribal elders who are the great masters of the proverb and the most fervent believers in its power. Enjoying the status of patriarchal sages,

they see themselves as the guardians of the clan's cultural heritage, much of which has been handed down in the form of proverbs .... This society does not regard the aged as a burden but rather as its venerable mentors who are expected to counsel and advise.[18]

The individualism which Obi expresses: "I am not going to listen to you anymore .... But don't you dare interfere in my affair again," is not compatible with the society that makes it the duty of elders to advise and when necessary admonish the young. As the Igbo adage states: "An old man does not watch a nanny-goat parturiate on the tetter." The society therefore enjoins the mutual appreciation of the role of elders by this and another adage that "seeing young people go astray without admonishing them is [causes] the death of elders but stubbornness and recalcitrance are [cause] the [premature] death of the young".The implication of which is, from the society's point of view, that without this guidance from elders the propagation of their cultural heritage cannot be assured; but more than that, it ensures both the conformity of the individual within the society and his acquisition of a proper sense of history. David Cook's comments quoted in the first section of this study succinctly express this world-view. As he says:

> In the traditional society the individual is seen first and foremost as part of a corporate whole, and his existence as part of the social pattern overwhelms any private life he might lead within the confines of his own consciousness. Such a life is relatively public: it is not easy to keep secrets nor is it thought desirable to do so. In such a situation, social conventions exert a great authority. The communal good is all-important and any personal denial of group commitment appears to weaken the whole and is deplored.

(Cook,p.4)

One must admit that Obi's attempts at individualism are heroic, particularly his stand on wanting to marry Clara in spite of her being an *osu* and against social convention, and the inconvenience of starting an immediate repayment to Umuofia Progressive Union of it's loan, albeit naive. The adage that, "an individual may cook a meal for the whole clan to eat [they will finish the food and still have the capacity to eat more] but if the clan as a whole cooks a meal for one person, the person will not be able to consume all" is an affirmation of the potency of clan solidarity, and an acknowledgement of the collective might of a united front. Obi in his quest for individualism had conveniently forgotten that issues like marriages and deaths in the traditional Igbo society are not private affairs but public matters, where often, the individuals concerned are relegated to the background. Again Cook makes the point that, "in a village there are very few places where an essentially private existence can be pursued. Contribution to the life and welfare of the community is the greatest good; and hence individualism is seen as negative"(Cook,p.4). The implacable stance of the society on the *osu* issue is enshrined in the words of Obi's father: "Osu is like leprosy in the minds of our people."

In pitching Obi against the society on a vital issue as the *osu* caste system, Achebe exposes one of the endemic injustices in Igbo culture and recognises that it is an issue that can only be overcome by the collective will of the people. Obi remarks that his "mind was troubled not only by what had happened but also by the discovery that there was nothing in him with which to challenge it honestly" (*NLE*, p.137). It is evident through Achebe's exposition, that Obi cannot rouse any :"righteous indignation", for the simple reason that his father's stance represents the views of the whole society. Achebe asserts this point most forcefully in *Arrow of God* when he concludes that "no man however great can win judgement against a clan".

But more relevant than the highlighting of these social injustices - the caste system, bribery, and extortion - is Achebe's exposure of Obi's ineffectualness in confronting these issues. Having portrayed the hopes that the society places on Obi and his class, Achebe systematically analyses how well this class fulfills those hopes, through Obi. Achebe views Obi's attempt at emancipation, in proclaiming his intention of marrying an *osu*, as a fatuous gesture. Not just because he failed to carry out his intentions, but more importantly, because he did not have the moral strength to stand by Clara in her time of need. Obi's action alienates him from friends and family, and destroys Clara's life, forcing her to prefer absconding rather than staying in Lagos.

Also when Obi, on his way to Umuofia, sees his chance to challenge corruption positively by confronting the policemen extorting money from drivers on the highway, all he does is stare at the policemen which results in the driver paying ten shillings instead of two shillings. All Obi does is mutter to himself: "What an Augean stable!"(*NLE*, p.43). It is pertinent that Obi does recognise that what the society needs is "even one man with vision", but he fails to see himself as a possible candidate (*NLE*, p.44).

Achebe believes that no meaningful democracy can exist in the face of such pervasive corruption: "But what kind of democracy can exist side by side with so much corruption and ignorance?"(*NLE*, p.44) It is precisely because of the "stinking nature of the Augean stable" which pervasive corruption represents, and the fact that it pervades all facets of public life, that Obi and his class were seen as the hope of the society, and of democracy. Obi in his analysis of "bribery in Nigeria's public life" had argued that the Nigerian public service was corrupt because the top positions were occupied by people who got to their present positions by bribery, and that it would remain so until the young graduates take over because, as he says: "To most of them bribery is no problem. They come straight to the top without bribing anyone. It's not that they're necessarily better than others, it's simply that they can afford to be virtuous. But even that kind of virtue can become a habit" (*NLE*, pp.20-1). Viewed from this perspective, Obi's action, his succumbing to corruption, assumes the significance of a betrayal. It is a betrayal of both the society that placed so much hope on him and his class, and of his theories; hence Achebe's (and the society's) disillusionment with this class.

Thus far, we have noted the demands and often contradictory expectations from Obi both by the Union, the extended family system, and the larger society. Given Achebe's characterisation of Obi as a weak man, it is my view that some of these demands are excessive. It requires more than an "ordinary" character to hold a balance between being sophisticated, urbane and "Europeanised", and retaining a meaningful foothold on one's cultural heritage. But Obi is an ordinary character. Gerald Moore and Arthur Ravenscroft have noted how "unheroic" and "simple-minded" Obi is: It is a very simple-minded young man indeed who does not expect to receive a demand for income tax or an electricity bill" (Ravenscroft, p.21). Achebe's sympathy for Obi, I believe, is not in the financial and materialistic demands made on him, for these (as has already been indicated) can be resolved by a careful balancing of "want and have", but in the emotional demands on him and the class he represents. That Obi's greatest dilemma is the resolution of the conflicting demands that he live and act like a "been-to" and at the same time retain the tribal mores has also been highlighted, but there is one other dimension which Oladele Taiwo observes:

Because members of the Union think of Obi's education as a means of protecting their own interests against the claims of others, they expect him as a senior Civil Servant to continue to share communal ideals and values, however limited in orientation, and to refrain from any assertion of his individualism"

(Taiwo,p.125).

Stifling of individualism is not compatible with Western education which, according to Taiwo, is "a means of self-improvement and individual growth".(Taiwo, p.125). The tragedy is that the traditional society did not appreciate the inherent psychological changes that go with formal education: "Neither the old colonial administration nor the traditional communal group can comprehend the strength of the forces at work on members of this young professional elite."[19] This is one of the issues that Achebe's *No Longer at Ease* highlights. Unfortunately, Obi cannot contain these tensions, neither does he communicate the problems he is facing adequately for them to be appreciated by those with whom he comes in contact.

It is pertinent at this point to remark Achebe's use of the proverb that, "if a finger brings oil, it soils the others" as an abiding principle in the Igbo world-view. It is this tendency for "evil"[20] to pollute whatever it comes in contact with that accounts for the vehemence with which everyone, including the elders of Umuofia Progressive Union, tries to dissuade Obi from marrying an *osu*, but all rally round him in times of trouble. The failure of Obi and the class he represents to fulfii the hopes and expectations of the society, like the oil in the proverb, has resulted in a perpetuation of such social evils as forbode a danger for democracy.

In *No Longer at Ease*, therefore, Achebe through Obi Okonkwo illustrates the lack of reponsibility, among other things, exhibited by the inheritors of the new nations of Africa, whose primary functions should have been to lay the concrete foundations for post-colonial developments but who, instead, "like the absurd man who was pursuing rats while his house was in flames", preferred to allow their houses to be razed rather than salvage what they can, by institutionalising corruption, graft, and tribalism (*MYCD*,p.78). By the time Achebe came to write *A Man of the People*, his pessimism had turned to despair at what "we have made of independence".

A Man of the People: Achebe's Despair with the Political Mess

A Man of the People brings Achebe's tetralogy up to the period from 1960 to 1966. Achebe, in an interview with Robert Serumaga soon after the publication of the novel, said that "every society has to grow up, every society has to learn its own lesson, so I don't despair".[21] But *A Man of the People* reflects Achebe's intense disillusionment with the way things had gone, and a general sense of despair at the mess that had been made of self-rule. Achebe in the same interview says that, "if it were for me to order society I would be very unhappy about the way things have turned out" and goes on to say categorically: "*A Man of the People* is a rather serious indictment . . . of post-independence Africa".[22] Neal Ascherson, writing specifically of *Anthills of the Savannah* says that instead of independence, when it came, fashioning "something modern and democratic" out of the existing social structure "in a slow, natural evolution", that as "so often [happens] although not everywhere, independence set off a degenerative process: freedom became corruption, while democracy collapsed into autocracy."[23]

In *No Longer at Ease* Achebe establishes that the emergent black administrative class who inherited the "new order" from the colonial administrators have exchanged the tribal traditional values for "new values". With *A Man of the People* Achebe indicates that they, along with their politician counterparts, have not been adequately socialized to appreciate all the dialectics that energise and make democratic governance meaningful. Wilfred Cartey writes that:

> Many of the characters and types presented in the urban political novels enter politics specifically for its lure, for the momentary glitter and glamor that accompany it, for the prestige and power it gives them. Entry into politics seems to destroy morality of any kind, transforming the politician into a self-seeking and unscrupulous activist .

(Cartey,p.158)

Achebe shows that such concepts as moral principles, tolerance for opposition, and most importantly the use of power for the benefit of the people do not have much meaning to the politicians as they scramble for the most lucrative offices and appointments. Odili's discussion with Max about the morality of a junior minister in government being involved in the formation of the new party, Common People's Convention, highlights this point:

> I knew very well and needed no reminder that we were not in Britain or something, that when a man resigned in our country it was invariably with an eye on the main chance - as when a few years ago ten newly elected P.A.P. Members of Parliament had switched parties at the opening of the session and given the P.O.P a comfortable majority overnight in return for ministerial appointments and - if one believed the rumours - a little cash prize each as well . . . . You take a man like Nanga now on a salary of four thousand plus all the - you know. You know what his salary was as an elementary school teacher? Perhaps not more than eight pounds a month. Now do you expect a man like that to resign on a little matter of principle. . . ?

(*AMOP*, p.93)

Achebe writes that both Odili himself and Chief Nanga knew that Nanga would win his electorate in the forthcoming election, with or without Odili's opposition. Odili says that: "Although I had little hope of winning Chief Nanga's seat, it was necessary nonetheless to fight and expose him as much as possible." Chief Nanga confirms that he was bound to win the election when he tells Odili: "I am not afraid of you. Every goat and every fowl in this country knows that you will fail woefully. You will lose your deposit and disgrace yourself." But despite this assured knowledge, Chief Nanga was not willing to tolerate any opposition at all, preferring to be elected unopposed as that would enhance his prestige at the capital and would also be an endorsement of the people's trust and confidence in him: "I am only giving you this money because I feel that after all my years of service to my people I deserve to be elected unopposed so that my detractors in Bori will know that I have my people solidly behind me"(*AMOP*, p.132).

Achebe indicates that the Nangas and the Kokos would stop at nothing; from bribery, through intimidation of the village people at large, to physical assault and battery to get what they want. And as Neal Ascherson notes in his review of *Anthills:* "During the years of open political contest, the first "independence" generation recklessly allowed the distinction between power and force to be blurred, until those whose trade was force began in increasing numbers to drive their tanks across that line."[24] To Nanga and his type, the wisdom of the ancients which advises tolerance among contestants, does not apply to politics. Odili's father states this need for tolerance through the Igbo proverb that: "I believe that the hawk should perch and the eagle perch, whichever says to the other don't,may its wing break." Chief Nanga's sinister and intimidating moves to ensure that he retains his seat in parliament, and consequently his ministerial position, typifies the problem with many new African nations:

> On top of that he has brought you two hundred and fifty pounds if you will sign this paper . . . . Chief Nanga moved swiftly and, as you would expect, ruthlessly . . . . It was announced that Mr Hezekiah Samalu, chairman of P.O.P. in Urua, has been 'ignominiously removed from his office for subversive, anti-party activities . . . . The next day . . . the local council Tax Assessment Officer brought him a reassessed figure based not only on his

known pension of eighty-four pounds a year but on an alleged income of five hundred pounds derived from 'business'. . . . The culmination came at the weekend when seven Public Works lorries arrived in the village and began to cart away the pipes they had deposited several months earlier for projected Rural Water Scheme.
(*AMOP*, pp.132,146-9)

Achebe has consistently maintained and defended the didactism of his writings. It is in the light of this overt intent that *A Man of the People* scrutinises what has gone wrong with both the Nigerian people and their rulers: "What we need to do is to look back and try and find out where we went wrong, where the rain began to beat us". He identifies four basic factors as responsible for the deplorable state of affairs and the resultant tensions. These factors, as Achebe's fiction indicates are: the lack of an adequate moral and ethical monitoring yardstick for the actions of people in politics, private greed, society's apathy, and lack of political vision, personal responsibility, and direction on the part of leaders.

Achebe's writings depict the situation that although the traditional society's culture is oral, the close-knit nature of the extended family and village systems ensures the accountability of tribal elders and leaders. But on a national level, the lack of precedence as functions in a traditional society on which the society could assess and judge the performances of their "leaders", means that the "new" leaders could do virtually anything they pleased without censure. The village code of ethics was powerless on a national level. As Odili says: "But in the affairs of the nation there was no owner, the laws of the village became powerless"(*NLE,* p.167). Achebe illustrates this powerlessness, as Carroll remarks, with the example of Josiah, whose behaviour to the blind man the tribal society found objectionable and proceeded to tell him so in no uncertain terms:

Unlike the village where unscrupulous Josiah is quickly and effectively outlawed, the country as a whole has no kind of political morality by which to judge and condemn a Nanga . . . . The results of this are the recurrent political and economic crises with which the events of the novel are punctuated".
(Carroll,p.130).

Achebe sees this lack of political morality as compounded by a lack of any meaningful objective criticism, the press having already abdicated this responsibility. It is for this reason that Achebe along with other writers believe that they, the writers, now have to perform this function as social critics. On this, Soyinka says: "When the writer in his own society can no longer function as conscience, he must recognise that his choice lies between denying himself totally or withdrawing to the position of chronicler and post-mortem surgeon."[25]

Achebe believes that another contributory factor to the post-colonial tensions of the society in the new nations is the tendency among those who find themselves in positions of power, to see those positions as their birthright. They therefore utilise any and every means to perpetuate themselves in such positions. Odili uses the metaphor of "the rain" to succintly expresses the driving impulse of personal greed and the hankering for power:

> The trouble with our new nation was that none of us had been indoors long enough to be able to say 'To hell with it.' We had all been in the rain together until yesterday. Then a handful of us - the smart and the lucky and hardly ever the best - had scrambled for the one shelter our former rulers left, and had taken it over and barricaded themselves in. And from within they had sought to persuade the rest through numerous loudspeakers, that the first phase of the struggle had been won and that the next phase - the extension of our house - was even more important and called for new and original tactics; it required that all argument should cease and the whole people speak with one voice and that any more dissent and argument outside the door of the shelter would subvert and bring down the whole house.
>
> *(AMOP*, p.42).

Achebe views this inclination to cling to power as arising from the lack of established ground rules, and the society's conception of what colonial and post-colonial politics means. To them it is not an extension of the traditional set-up, particularly as the traditional Igbo societies did not recognise nor invest individuals with absolute powers to control the society's destiny. Achebe's astute depiction of the distance that exists between those who wielded authority in traditional society and the colonial administration in both *Things Fall Apart* and *Arrow of God,* and his comment that the Christian church first attracted the *efulefu* and societal outcasts is important. Its importance lies in the colonial administration's method of choosing those they invested with authority. Achebe gives an example of this in *Arrow of God*:

> Three years ago they had put pressure on Captain Winterbottom to appoint a Warrant Chief for Okperi . . . . After a long palaver he had chosen one James Ikedi, an intelligent fellow who had been among the very first people to receive missionary education in these parts . . . . The man was a complete nonentity until we crowned him, and now he carries on as though he had been nothing else all his life.
>
> (*AOG*, pp.57,107)

Achebe's fiction consistently suggests that these characters who were functioning as links between the colonialists and the indigenous people - interpreters, government clerks, warrant chiefs, and court messengers among others - were famous for their high-handedness and were consequently hated. Odili relates one of such experiences: "But it was not until many years later that I caught one fleeting, terrifying glimpse of just how hated an Interpreter could be" (*AMOP*, p.33). He goes further to explain that his friend's father on learning that Odili was the son of Hezekiah Samalu, "a retired District Interpreter" told him quite bluntly: "Then you cannot stay in my house. . . .I don't blame you, my son, or you either, because no one has told you. But know it from today that no son of Hezekiah Samalu's shelters under my roof" (*AMOP*, pp.33-4). This reaction of the people to these government functionaries created a gulf between the two sets of people, and Achebe's writings further suggest that the society at the point of contact saw such characters as Chief Ikedi, nonentities who were created by the "new order", as symbols of colonialism and oppression. Achebe believes that since most of the early converts were *efulufus* and outcasts, they would have no regard for the culture of that society, but most importantly they would have no compunction to oppress the society which had hitherto looked upon them with contempt, and this would in turn be reflected on the relationship between the colonial administration and the indigenous people. Achebe illustrates this further through Chief Ikedi:

> Within three months of this man receiving his warrant Captain Winterbottom began to hear rumours of his high-handedness. He had set up an illegal court and a private prison. He took any woman who caught his fancy without paying the customary brideprice. Captain Winterbottom went into the whole business thoroughly and uncovered many more serious scandals .... The latest thing he did was to get his people to make him an Obi or king, so that he was now called His Highness Ikedi the First, Obi of Okperi. This among a people who abominated kings! This was what British administration was doing among the Ibos, making a dozen mushroom kings grow where there was none before.
>
> (*AOG*, pp.57-8)

This "distance" is also exemplified by the comments of Edna's mother when she is told that Odili is contesting Chief Nanga's seat: "She listened carefully, thought about it and then said: 'What is my share in that? They are both white man's people. And they know what is what between themselves. What do we know?'" (*AMOP*, p.119) This apparent unconcern typifies the society's attitude to national politics. To them it is the "white man's" system, an innovation that came with colonialism, even when as since independence, it is their son's and daughter's who are ruling. Achebe sees this non-identification with the political system by the society; and the concept of seeing it as no concern of theirs as having resulted in a general apathy to whatever goes on.

The cynicism of the people is the product of the foregoing issues, and more. From the outset, most of those who were given the warrant to rule saw it as an opportunity, in an acquisitive society, to become rich. Having set the trend and, given the protection of "their creators" these emergent black "rulers" and administrators waxed strong. Winterbottom, smarting from his superiors over-riding his decision about Chief Ikedi states: "But after three months, the Senior Resident who had just come back from leave and had no first-hand knowledge of the matter ruled that the rascal [Chief Ikedi] be reinstated. And no sooner was he back in power than he organized a vast system of mass extortion" (*AOG*, p.57). Achebe believes that it is for this reason also that they would do anything to perpetuate themselves in power. So the society comes to see being in power as a short cut to riches:

> The first thing critics tell you about our ministers' official residences is that each has seven bedrooms and seven bathrooms, one for every day of the week .... I was simply hypnotized by the luxury of the great suite assigned to me. When I lay down in the double bed that seemed to ride on a cushion of air, and switched on that reading lamp and saw all the beautiful furniture . . . the gleaming bathroom and the towels as large as a lappa I had to confess that if I were that moment made a minister I would be most anxious to remain one for ever.
> (*AMOP*, pp.41-2)

Eldred Jones writes that the central concern of *A Man of the People,* "is the cynicism of both the politicians and the people which brings about a situation that invites intervention. The politicians cynically use their positions to enrich themselves at the expense of the people, while the people, with the philosophy born of despair tamely lie down under the imposition."[26]

Achebe makes the point that to the people the two systems of government - traditional and colonial - are seen as diametrically at variance. Chief Nanga, Chief Ikedi and their like wield almost absolute power over the lives of the society, to which the society has no (or thinks it has no) recourse to redress: since their oppressors control the system of law, the press, and ultimately dictate the terms of their governance. Conversely, in the traditional society the people themselves have a say in what happens, and how their lives are to be governed. Morality is held in high regard and the actions of individuals and the society are motivated by what they feel is in the interest of the community. The traditional mores and beliefs foster the social and moral ethics ensuring mutual co-existence of all. Even outcasts, though socially discriminated against, are also given some form of protection. Molesting of their person, for example, is taboo and in some societies any member of the community who so much as causes an outcast to bleed without the express injunction of the gods performs certain prohibitive propitiatory rites.

But most importantly, the system of government is intrinsically interwoven with these mores. In Achebe's writings the ancestors are seen to be ever present and watchful through the interactions and the presence of the *egwuegwu, mmo,* priests and priestesses. Quarrels are settled not by any strict adherence to right and wrong, or censure, but by such compromises as are necessary and required to maintain intra-communal fellowship. Paradoxically such settlements, which must be accomplished on the basis of a detailed knowledge of tradition, must also be flexible enough to accommodate the ever changing needs of the society as a living structure.

Achebe particularly shows the mechanics by which the society controls its own governance. He indicates that individuals are allowed to have their say in matters of general concern (*TFA*, p.11). Individuals who disagree with any verdict reached by the society have access to a superior authority for redress, as shown by the land and domestic disputes settlement scenes in *Things Fall Apart.* The society acknowledges that such individuals could bring such matters (even trivial ones) to the assembly of only the titled elders. If they are still not satisfied, or the matter gets beyond the titled elders the individual has recourse to the powers of the ancestral spirits through the invocation of the *egwuegwu.* Since these are representatives of the spirit world and founders of the clan, the general belief is that they are beyond bias. Even though no one could be imagined as refusing to abide by the decisions of the ancestral spirits, yet lurking behind this formidable arbiters are the gods and goddesses themselves to whose shrines any individuals who are sore pressed could bring their supplications and cases, as the ultimate arbiters. However, any one getting this far realised that they are in the realm of spirits, and transgression has sometimes only one penalty, death. The belief being that one would be foolhardy to allow matters to get this far without being satisfied: "'I don't know why such a trifle should come before the egwugwu,' said one elder to another. 'Don't you know what kind of man Uzowulu is? He will not listen to any other decision,' replied the other" (*TFA*,85). This is a major reason that despite the presence of this other avenue to the society, no one allows disputes to get so out of hand that its final resolution can only be at the feet of a god or goddess. Achebe sees the workings of these checks and balances as curbing peoples' inherent tendency for excesses. Even a character such as Nwaka in *Arrow of God*, with all his wealth and exaggerated antagonism for Ezeulu is also conscious of the power of the gods and while he throws his challenges, deliberately couches his language in such a way that he could not be said to have challenged Ulu personally. But more relevant is that as one of the leaders of the clan, Nwaka is doing what he feels is for the good of the community. He fears, and Achebe agrees, with good reason that Ezeulu was trying to usurp the powers of the clan to determine their destiny. He gives one of his reasons for wanting the clan to war against Okperi as stemming from a desire to avoid Umuaro being seen by other communities as too weak to protect its lands. Other reasons notwithstanding, he cannot be accused of not having the good of Umuaro at heart from this perspective. Even some of Ezeulu's convoluted reasons for not eating the sacred yams, or announcing the new season, could be seen, probably in a twisted way, to be out of interest for the clan: for if he eats the yam, he would transgress, and Ulu in punishing him may punish the clan.

But no such soul-searching, or community-oriented thinking governs the actions of the black administrators and leaders. They approach their responsibility with what the society sees as "chop-make-I-chop" philosophy. Achebe believes that they have substituted the erstwhile colonial administration with a more insidious form of government. Achebe's depiction of Chief Nanga exemplifies the corruption, graft, tribalistic patronage, and the undermining of such democratic principles as free press and competition which most African nations are afflicted with. As Wilfred Cartey says:

> The chicanery, folly, corruption, and violence of a changing political order are at the center of the novel, A Man of the People, .
> . . . Practical politics on the local level, its inner workings and

functions, are all presented through the central figure, Chief Honorable M. A. Nanga, M.P., a satirical portrait of one of the many new ministers who control the reins of government in many of the developing countries.

(Cartey,pp.147-8)

The narrative opens with Achebe portraying Chief Nanga's affability, and the society extolling his virtues:

> No one can deny that Chief the Honourable M. A. Nanga, M.P., was the most approachable politician in the country. Whether you asked in the city or in his home village, Anata, they would tell you he was a man of the people . . . . She was now praising Micah's handsomeness, which she likened to the perfect, sculpted beauty of a carved eagle, and his popularity which would be the envy of the proverbial traveller-to- distant-places who must not cultivate enmity on his route.
>
> (*AMOP*, p.1)

But Achebe undercuts this benign exterior with a critique of the political mess which Chief Nanga and his colleagues have made of self-government:

> The arrival of the members of the hunters' guild in full regalia caused a great stir . . . . These people never came out except at the funeral of one of their number, or during some very special and outstanding event . . . . Occasionally a hunter would take aim at a distant palm branch and break its mid-rib . . . . But there were very few such shots. Most of the hunters reserved their precious powder to greet the Minister's arrival - the price of gunpowder like everything else having doubled again and again in the four years since this government took control.
>
> (*AMOP*, pp.1-2)

Odili's initial disillusionment, as Achebe shows, is an outcome of the lack of principle, and the brazen selfishness with which those in power approached the responsibility of self-rule. Achebe illustrates this through the feral imagery with which Odili qualifies Chief Nanga and his associates. Achebe writes that Mr Nanga as "an unknown back-bencher in the governing P.O.P", with some of his colleagues "seeing the empty ministerial seats, had yapped and snarled so shamelessly for the meaty prize". Continuing Odili, the narrator, says that:

> Throughout the session he led the pack of back-bench hounds straining their leash to get at their victims. If any one had cared to

sum up Mr Nanga's interruptions they would have made a good hour's continuous yelp. Perspiration poured down his face as he sprang up to interrupt or sat back to share in the derisive laughter of the hungry hyena.

(*AMOP*, pp5-6)

Through such imagery as "hounds", "dogs", "yelp", "straining their leash",'yapped and snarled", and "hyena", Achebe creates a looming and foreboding image of the emergent black administrators and leaders which Chief Nanga and his political colleagues typify, but also which portends the "death" of the new nations of Africa.

Underlying Chief Nanga's suave appearance Achebe portrays a calculating ruthlessness bordering on unscrupulousness. Apart from Chief Nanga's intolerance for any form of competition and his resort to bribery, and physical assaults on his opponents, he is depicted as seeing himself as accountable to no one, not even to his electorate. He blatantly uses his position to intimidate both his opponents and to blackmail the larger society, his electorate. Achebe indicates a society caught in a hopeless situation, and which is at the mercy of its leaders. Odili states that:

> Two nights later we heard the sound of the Crier's gong. His message was unusual. In the past the Crier had summoned the village to a meeting to deliberate over a weighty question, or else to some accustomed communal labour. His business was to serve notice of something that was to happen. But this night he did something new: he announced a decision already taken. The elders and the councillors of Urua and the whole people, he said, had decided that in the present political fight raging in the land, they should make it known that they knew one man and one man alone - Chief Nanga. Every man and every woman in Urua and every child and every adult would throw his or her paper for him on the day of the election . . . . And I thought: if the whole people had taken the decision why were they being told of it?

(*AMOP*, p.151)

Odili's doubts reflect the manner in which incumbents in power usurp "the power of the people". The people's fear of playing the role of sacrificial ram and losing their share of the "national cake" drives the village to recant their earlier decision to support their son because Chief Nanga, as the Igbos say, "has the yam and the knife".[27] Odili's comments that: "I couldn't say I blamed my village people from recoiling from the role of sacrificial ram. Why should they lose their chance of getting good, clean water, their share of the national cake? In fact they had adequate justification for their *volte-face* just two days later when the pipes returned" (*AMOP*, pp.151-2). Such unscrupulous misuse of power is indicative of Achebe's emphatic indictment of post-colonial African leaders of whom Chief Nanga is typical. By demonstrating Chief Nanga's far-reaching powers of intimidation (of the society), Achebe as Carroll acknowledges, shows that "there is a disastrous fracture between the morality of the village and the political affairs of the nation" (Carroll,p.150). The various instances of Chief Nanga's apparent control and manipulation of the Press, from his giving a "'dash' of five pounds" to the greasy-looking editor, to his remarks to the Minister of Public Construction: "Don't worry about the Press; I will make sure that they don't publish it" (*AMOP*, pp.47-8), reinforces Achebe's disillusionment with national politics.

While Achebe's disillusionment can be attributed to witnessing the adverse effects of the unscrupulousness of the actions of "the Chief Nangas" in government on the new nations, he is also critical of the society for its cynicism and apathy. Apart from the lack of precedents and ground rules on which the society could base its assessment of its leaders, Achebe is also concerned with the general trend of seeing political offices and appointments as short cuts to riches, as already discussed in this chapter. But an extension of this misconception is the society's motive for supporting candidates. Achebe believes that at the beginning the society saw politics as part of the package which came with colonialism. He states that change came with the realisation that politics carried an attendant fabulous cash prize: "Nanga must have gone into politics soon afterwards and then won a seat in Parliament. It was easy in those days - before we knew its cash price" (*AMOP*, p.3).

And so in spite of Chief Nanga's massive support in his electorate, the people of Urua decided to cast their votes to Odili. This is not because they see him as a better candidate to Chief Nanga, nor that he has an alternative political ideology and vision, but because he is their son. They see his entry into politics as automatically drawing them nearer to the plate, and so affording them an easier reach at the cake. Max, arguing on why Odili's village people should vote for him, states: "Last time you elected a member of parliament from Anata. Now it is your turn here in Urua. A goat does not eat into a hen's stomach no matter how friendly the two may be. Ours is ours but mine is mine" (*AMOP*, p.140). Achebe sees Max's speech and the old man's remarks as the bane of the politics of the new nations of Africa:

> There is one word he said which entered my ear more than everything else . . . . That word was that our own son should go and bring our share . . . . The village of Anata has already eaten, now they must make way for us to reach the plate. No man in Urua will give his paper to a stranger when his own son needs it; if the very herb we go to seek in the forest now grows at our back yard are we not saved the journey? We are ignorant people and we are like children. But I want to tell our son one thing . . . anyone who wants to look at our new tooth should know that his bag should be heavy.
>
> (*AMOP*, p.141)

But Odili's father sums up this attitude. In spite of the gulf of antagonism between him and his son, he willingly supports Odili believing that he now has come to appreciate the necessity of "joining the rat race": "When you came home with a car I thought to myself: good, some sense is entering his belly at last. . . . But I should have known . . . . If the money he was offering was too small why did you not say so? Why did you not ask for three or four hundred?" (*AMOP*, p.135). This criticism of Odili from his father for refusing Chief Nanga's bribe and stepping down from the political race, indicates that nothing but the financial and material rewards of politics is of importance to the society. In Achebe's view, as David Carroll says, the national interest will always come second to this society.[28]

While Achebe indicts those in power for their self-seeking propagation of tribalism and ethnicism, for their politics of intimidation and blackmail; and the people for their cynic acquiescence in the muddle, he also criticises "the Odilis" and "the Maxes" for their lack of political vision and direction. Michael Neill, making basically the same point, says: "At the end of *[A Man of the People]* its protagonist-narrator, Odili the great, may have lived to triumph over his corrupt political and sexual adversary, Chief Nanga, but in the light of all that he has revealed about his own deeply equivocal relation to the 'eat-and-let-eat regime just ended', Odili's rhetoric of political awakening sounds a slightly hollow note."[29]

Achebe sees both Max, Odili, and their new political party, CPC., as not providing any meaningful new sense of political direction, likening it as the ex-policeman, Couple, did to a third vulture: "There were three vultures, . . . the third and youngest was called CPC" (*AMOP*, p.140). Odili's remarks to Max that: "I would have thought it was better to start our new party, with a different kind of philosophy" implies that "Couple" was right in seeing CPC. as another vulture. Also Odili's reaction on first learning that a "junior minister in the Government was behind" the formation of the new party exemplifies Achebe's outrage at their lack of moral principle. Max's rationalisation of both the man's presence in the party and his own acceptance of bribe from Chief Koko only confirms Achebe's feeling that democracy as an institution has become so abused that the formation of a new political party does not offer any remedy. Achebe stated in the interview with Robert Serumaga that:

> If you take the example of Nigeria, which is the place I know best, things had got to such a point politically that there was no other answer - no way you could resolve this impasse politically. The political machine had been so abused that whichever way you pressed it, it produced the same results; and therefore you wanted another force, another force just had to come in.[30]

Achebe equates a new political party founded on corruption Max accepts bribes, Odili borrows party funds for non-party purposes at will) with still-birth as exemplified by Max's death. Eustace Palmer argues that given the same chance as Nanga,

Odili would, in all probability become another Chief Nanga and writes: "The true subject of this novel is not really political corruption, but the corrupting power of privilege, position, and money."[31] He goes on to add that "the interest lies in . . . the process whereby the supposedly idealistic Odili gradually succumbs to the temptations of political success and starts to resemble, in attitude at least, Chief Nanga himself" (Palmer,p.73).

A Man of the People thus symbolised for Achebe, a reappraisal of what has been made of an independence that he feels was without substance, in the first place: "This is the beginning of a phase for me in which I intend to take a hard look at what we in Africa are making of independence - but using Nigeria which I know best."[32] It represented along with *No Longer at Ease*, an end to the age of pastoral writing, and of innocence. As Ngugi points out: "What Achebe has done in *A Man of the People* [and *No Longer at Ease*] is to make it impossible or inexcusable for other African writers to do other than address themselves directly to [contemporary social realities] their audience in Africa . . . and tell them that such problems are their concern."[33] Achebe by confronting these post-colonial tensions, by moving "with a whip among the pupils, flagellating himself as well as them", is demonstrating and setting some critical standards by which the society could assess their hitherto irrepressible leaders.[34] Henceforth, he is saying, the society can tell when their leaders "have taken enough for the owner to see" (*AMOP*, p.166).

But Achebe's long silence after *A Man of the People*, and his comment that even if he wanted he couldn't write a novel now; that he could only write essays or poems: short and intense works in keeping with his mood illustrate the depth of his despair at the bastardization of the political legacy which has occurred.[35]

CHAPTER FOUR

The Unwanted Seer: Achebe's Short Stories, Poems of War and Recent Fiction

The Still Birth of a Dream; Achebe's Short Stories and Poems on the Nigerian Civil War

That Achebe's social consciousness has been a motivating factor in his writing has been established in the course of this analysis. That he also believes the Nigerian political machinery to have been abused, possibly beyond remedy, has also become evident. In his essay, "The Black Writer's Burden" (1966), Achebe passionately implores African writers and critics to face the "first real challenge" that the continent is witnessing - to criticise the corruption and misrule which he sees as rife in the continent without flinching. Both *No longer at Ease* and *A Man of the People* are attempts to do this. Achebe, talking to Serumaga in 1967 about the resolution of the political impasse in *A Man of the People* remarks "Now when I was writing *A Man of the People* it wasn't clear to me that this was going to be necessarily a military intervention. It could easily have been civil war, which in fact it very nearly was in Nigeria".[1.] He goes on to say:

> But I think that all these things the next generation of politicians in Nigeria, when we do have them, will have experienced, and they'll have learned one or two lessons, I hope, from what happened to the First Republic. This is the only hope I have and if it turns out to be vain, it would really be terrible. [2]

That civil war finally eventuated was both a vindication of the seer's prophetic vision, and his realistic analysis of contemporary political trends which he says was evident as far back as 1964. "And the indication of how politics was going to develop in Nigeria was there already. If you cared to look, I think the signs were everywhere."[3] Achebe sees the death of democracy as being a consequence of the lack of responsibility already highlighted and believed that the Biafran revolution (1967-1970) provided a chance for Africans to lay a political foundation that is authentically egalitarian and based on philosophies "which took into account their present conditions".[4] Achebe in an interview in 1969, saw the Biafrian issue as, "a revolution that aims toward true independence, that moves toward the creation of modern states in place of the new colonial enclaves we have today, a revolution that is informed with African ideologies."[5]

Achebe's deepened disillusionment, as reflected in his short stories and poems, is consequent upon the failure of this dream. Contrary to the criticism made by Kolawole Ogungbesan, Achebe does not see the failure of the Biafrian revolution as an isolated case, despite his personal involvement in the crisis, but as another instance in a succession of squandered opportunities.[6] In his recent essay, "Where the Problem Lies",which is contained in his political booklet *The Trouble with Nigeria*, Achebe writes that: "The fear that should nightly haunt our leaders (but does not) is that they may already have betrayed irretrievably Nigeria's high destiny".[7] Having shown in the earlier fictions, that many of the excesses of the protagonists arise in part from their inability to use the powers and positions entrusted to them responsibly, and that the apathetic populace are also to blame for the derailing of the machinery, Achebe's short stories and poems show how the gross abuse of power and privilege by the elites of Africa's new nations destroy even the best dreams. While the first section of this chapter on the short stories and poems expose Achebe's intense disillusionment and bitterness at these wasted opportunites, the second section will explore his most recent fiction, and the "conditional" hope it embodies.

Achebe's short stories span a period of twenty years and many of them traverse areas already covered by his novels. "The Voter", as Carroll notes,"belongs to the world of *A Man of the People*", with the "Vengeful Creditor" and "Girls at War", they "diagnose the corruption of both private and public morality" (Carroll, p 162). In these stories Achebe astutely sketches those same destructive forces at work as were evident in the urban political novels. Carroll comments that some of Achebe's writings show his bitterness, particularly at "the absurd rituals of the unscrupulous parliamentarians and the double talk of the obsequious newspapers" (Carroll,p.163). The stories "Civil Peace" and "Girls at War" broaden, and paradoxically, heighten Achebe's bitterness and disillusionment. These short stories and poems, while testifying to the shattering of this dream, reflect "a society [and dream] that had gone completely rotten and maggoty at the centre".[8] Arthur Ravencroft says of "Girls at War", that it "has much the same bitterness as *A Man of the People,* though now modified by a deep sense of pity of lost ideals and untold derelictions".[9] The Biafrian experience in Achebe's view, is the obverse side of the same coin - a repetition of the same vicious circle of "untold derelictions" as plague the Nigerian state. The same unbridled materialism and selfishnesss that his earlier writings criticised, were evident and rife, even within the constraint of a civil war. Using the change in Gladys, from an initial nationalistic idealism to a realist, willing to do anything to survive the war as example, Nwankwo states that:

> There must be some man at the centre of it [the corruption of Gladys, perhaps one of those heartless traders who traffic in foreign currencies and make their hundreds of thousands by sending young men to hazard their lives bartering looted goods for cigarettes behind enemy lines, or one of those contractors who receive piles of money daily for food they never deliver to the army. Or perhaps some vulgar and cowardly army officer full of filthy barrack talk and fictitious stories of heroism.
>
> (*GAW*, p.114)

The same corruption and graft were now compounded by the fact that people were unscrupulously willing to manipulate human hunger and near starvation to their advantage:

> As his driver loaded tins and bags and cartons into his car the starved crowds that perpetually hung around relief centres made crude, ungracious remarks like 'War Can Continue!' meaning WCC! Nwankwo was deeply embarrassed not by the jeers of this scarecrow crowd of rags and floating ribs but by the independent accusation of their wasted bodies and sunken eyes.
>
> (*GAW*, p.102)

"Civil Peace", and particularly "Girls at War" illustrate this corruption, selfishness unbridled materialism and the death of a dream.

Achebe's "Civil Peace", Ravenscroft believes, is a celebration of the resilience of the human spirit with Jonathan's constant refrain of "nothing puzzles God", but it is also a remark at the level of societal degeneration.[10] To Jonathan Iwegbu, the miracle of surviving the war with his family is occasion for praising God:

> 'Happy survival!' meant so much more to him than just a current fashion of greeting old friends in the first hazy days of peace. It went deep to his heart. He had come out of the war with five inestimable blessings - his head, his wife Maria's head and the heads of three out of their four children. As a bonus he also had his old bicycle - a miracle too but naturally not to be compared to the safety of five human heads.
>
> (*GAW*,p.90)

And finding his house still standing albeit with missing doors, windows, and some roofing sheets, was another miracle. While Achebe explored the optimistic fatalism of this charater, he subtly analyses the brutalities of the war: "It wasn't his disreputable rags, nor the toes peeping out of the one blue and one brown canvas shoes . . . many good and heroic soldiers looked the same or worse"(*GAW*, p,90). But the story particularly highlights the prevalent dishonesty which neither the suffering occasioned by the war, nor the abject poverty of the survivors could deter some from practising: "He had to be extra careful because he had seen a man a couple of days earlier collapse in near madness in an instant before that oceanic crowd because no sooner had he got his twenty pounds than some ruffian picked it off him " (*GAW*, p.93).

As in his earlier fictions, Achebe indicts the society for its apathy. The comic charade of the robbers, from their cool announcement of their presence and who they are, to their helping Jonathan and his family raise the alarm of their presence, once more demonstrates the "spinelessness" of the society (neighbours). While Achebe highlights the heartlessness of the robbers, in depriving this poor family of their "egg-rasher", he criticises the society in which no one raised a finger to help a fellow in need of assistance - a society in which robbers have the boldness and audacity to raise an alarm of their own presence, knowing that no one would have the guts to do anything.

Achebe's "Girls at War" looks at some of the internal tensions that destroyed the spirit of a revolutioon, highlighting the

"maggoty centre". Achebe contrasts Gladys' initial zeal at the outset of the revolution with Reginald Nwankwo's hypocrisy:
> That was in the first heady days of warlike preparation when thousands of young men (and sometimes women too) were daily turned away from the enlistment centres because far too many of them were coming forward burning with readiness to bear arms in defence of the exciting new nation.
>
> (*GAW*, p98).

Carroll writes that through the eyes of Reginald Nwankwo,"We see the transformation of Gladys from her early military idealism in the Biafran cause through a period of uneasy normality to the simple and realistic desire for survival" (*Carroll*, p.164). Achebe through narrating the second encounter between Reginald and Gladys at a checkpoint, explores the pretentiousness of the highly placed who, despite the circumstances of a war, were still engaged in a dialectics of status, privilege and hypocrisy:
> Although intellectually he approved of thorough searches at roadblocks, emotionally he was always offended whenever he had to submit to them. He would probably not admit it but the feeling people got was that if you were put through a search then you could not really be one of the big people.
>
> (*GAW*, p.98)

Reginald admits that Gladys "wasn't going to make an exception even for one who once did her a favour. He was sure she would have searched her own father just as rigorously" *GAW*, pp. 100-1). Her subsequent degeneration, Reginald believes, could only be a result of the corrupting influences of those in positions of authority, who were using their positions (just as he himself does) to accumulate scarce commodities for themselves, their families, and their scores of girlfriends:
> When their paths crossed a third time. . . things had got very bad. Death and starvation having long chased out the headiness of the early days, now left in some places blank resignation, in others a rock-like, even suicidal, defiance. But surprisingly enough there were many at this time who had no other desire than to corner whatever good things were still going and to enjoy themselves to the limit . . . Reginald Nwankwo lived in Owerri then. But that day he had gone to Nkwerr[e] in search of relief. . .So he went now to see an old friend who ran the WCC depot at Nkwerri to get other items like rice, beans and that excellent cereal commonly called Gabon gari
>
> (*GAW*, p.101)

Reginald Nwankwo's self-righteous hypocrisy contrasts with his analysis of what has happened to Gladys within the two years of the war. Carroll views "Girls at War" as attempting a diagnosis of social malaise by means of its ironic structure, in that Reginald Nwankwo self-righteously seeks to understand the problems that he and people like him have caused. While he picks and chooses what type of food, from the pile he amasses from his sources, is terrible stuff and which is excellent in the midst of the starving masses, and goes to parties (but feels it is a sin to dance while the war lasts), picks up a young lady from the scorching sun while leaving an old woman behind, he still intellectually analyses the "tragedy" of the change that had taken place in Gladys.

Gladys however sees the issue of her change in very simple terms: "Now everybody wants survival. They call it number six. You put your number six, I put my number six. Everything all right" (*GAW*, p.109). But in Achebe's views, both characters, Reginald and Gladys, mirror the rottenness of the society in their different ways. Reginald reflects the corrupting influence of those in positions of authority who are only out to enjoy themselves. They even perpetuate the misery of thousands of their fellows in the process; they garner all the good relief materials to the detriment of the starving population. They frivolously engage in parties using the same food materials which they have deprived the people of:

> He hated the parties to which his friends clung like drowning men. And to talk so approvingly of them because he wanted to take a girl home! And this particular girl too, who had once had such beautiful faith in the struggle and was betrayed (no doubt about it) by some men like him out for a good time.
>
> (*GAW*, p.106)

Gladys herself is a reflection, as Reginald says of a society that has gone all rotten and maggoty at the centre:

> With a down-to-earth immediacy she responds directly to changing circumstances: in her idealistic phase she searches cars methodically, later she is ready to profit from the black market, is terrified of the bombing, gives her sexual favours casually, and throughout accepts the inevitability of hardship and injustice; 'Monkey de work, baboon de chop'"
>
> (*GAW*, p.114)

Kolawole Ogungbesan's critique "Politics and the African Writer" (1974), while generally critical of Achebe's emotiveness in the poems and short stories dealing with the war, is however, right in his assessment that some of these short stories and poems "show a closeness of observation and intense emotional involvement in the situation . . . Achebe has minutely recapitulated the ugly facts of life in Biafra during and immediately after the war."[11] The disillusionment after *A Man of the People*, and the eventual civil war, had left Achebe embittered, and the poems contained in *Beware Soul Brother* (1972), as Carroll says, "constitute a moving account of the poet's experience during this period and a searching examination of his role after the fighting has ended" (Carroll, p. 168).

Achebe attempts, in some of the poems, to evaluate the events prior to, during, and after the war. In "1966" and "The First Shot" Achebe explores the antecedent events to the war. He sees the necessity of this casual appraisal in the Igbo adage that: "But fighting will not begin unless there is first a thrusting of fingers into eyes. Anybody who wants to outlaw fights must first outlaw the provocation of fingers thrust into eyes"(*Anthills*, p 228). Contrary to Philip Rogers suggestion that "The First Shot" refers to 'The First Shot' of the evolution . . ." it is a reference to the causal anonymous "first shot" which, like the thrusting of fingers into eyes, causes fights.[12] Achebe infers that while memories of the actual civil war, "the greater noises" would fade, even its brutalising effects and scars forgotten, that the actions that preceded the war, "that lone rifle-shot",, even though anonymous, will yet, ever be remembered "lodge/more firmly. . ./ in the forehead of memory"(*BSB*,p.11). Rogers is, however, right that "its human motion suggests the steady accretion of purposes and accidents which make up wars' beginnings."[13]

As in "The First Shot", "1966" explores the destructive forces that led to the civil war. Achebe views the levity of the intelligentsia as a contributory factor. While they, who should know, absent-mindedly and thoughtlessly fixed their gazes on other things, "absentminded/our thoughtless days", and "played indolently", forces were already surreptitiously at work, "subterranean shaft", rousing jealousy and hatred between brothers, "rare artesian hatred", resulting as between Cain and Abel, in brother killing his brother "that once squirled warm/ blood in God's face" (*BSB*, p.3).

Carroll writes that the "Poems about War which follow in the next section range from the laconic 'Air Raid', where the man 'is much too slow' crossing the road and is cut in two by a bomb, through the bitterness at civilian suffering to relief when hostilities cease" (Carroll, p 170). While these poems about war graphi-cally reveal the sufferings and casualties of the war, in "Beware Soul Brother" and "Non-Commitment" Achebe re-examines the artist's role in the society, and the issue of commitment. Rogers believes that,"'Men of soul' is obviously intended to suggest artists, intellectuals, teachers, perhaps even politicians, the sense of the poem suggests, however, that he has his fellow-writers chiefly in mind."[14] Earlier in his analysis Rogers says that "In the central metaphor of the poem, writers are dancers; the earth of the dancing ground is their inspiration and their responsibility."[15] Achebe once more admonishes his fellow-writers, reminding them of their social commitment:

> The meaning of both the writer's soaring away from the earth and returning to it is suggested in Achebe's recent speeches, in which he expresses the fear that African writers, in their preoccupation with defending and displaying the past, have become disengaged from the earth, 'that zone of occult instability where the people dwell', and where 'the regenerative powers of the people are most potent'. Like a dance, the earth moves in time; if the writer falls behind, he will suffer the fate of the mango seedling trapped in elevated objectivity with no place for its roots. Or in the metaphor of 'Beware Soul Brother', he will 'become/a dancer disinherited in mid-dance/hanging a lame foot in the air like the hen/in a strange unfamiliar compound'.[16]

Achebe believes that even the mistakes of the past are valuable, if we learn a lesson by them: "We have/come to know from the surfeit of suffering/that even the Cross need not be a dead end nor total loss"; and that whatever beauties a dancer's feet may weave in the air, it must return to earth for regeneration and safety (*BSB*, p.29). This, he cautions his fellow artists to remember, for it is the reason that "Our ancestors" in their wisdom "gave Ala, great goddess /of the earth, sovereignty too over/their arts" (*BSB*, p.29). Failure to live up to their social responsibilities would lead to abandoning "our soils" to "the long ravenous tooth/and talon of" those who lie "in wait/ . . . only for the deep entrails".(*BSB*, p.29)

"Non-commitment" partly addresses the consequences of non-commitment, and as Rogers notes, "The uncommitted are represented as emotionally sterile, cut off literally in the metaphor of [the poem] from the possibility of regeneration because their 'hearts are fitted with prudence/ like a diaphragm across/ womb's beckoning doorway to bar/ the scandal of seminal rage.'"17 Critics, such as Kolawole Ogungbesan, Ali Mazrui and John Pepper Clark, have taken Achebe and Okigbo to task for their social consciousness and commitment which drove a poet such as Okigbo to forsake his pen in exchange for the gun. Clark, talking to Bernth Lindfors in 1969, declared: "I repeat, the role of the poet is to create poems, and you don't have to go and carry a gun to create a poem about war."18 Ogungbesan berates Achebe for becoming so involved in the fate of this society "as to put forward solutions to the problems facing his people".19 Achebe's poem, "Non-commitment", not only justifies the writer's need for social commitment, illustrating the atrophying consequences of non-commitment but it also echoes Soyinka's comments quoted earlier that: "When the writer in his own society can no longer function as conscience, he must recognise that his choice lies between denying himself totally or withdrawing to the position of chronicler and post-mortem surgeon".20

Re-formism as a Possible Solution to the Post-colonial Problems of Africa's New Nations" Achebe's Recent Fiction

While some of Achebe's short stories and poems have attempted to fill the void created by his "silence" after *A Man of the People* (1966), they have also shown the awakening and shattering of Achebe's dream of an authentic African new nation in the still-birth that was Biafra. Achebe's latest novel, *Anthills of the Savannah* (1987), extends his structural time sequence to the present. It encapsulates both Achebe's original views and concepts on the role of the artist in African societies, as contained in his earlier fictions and essays, his disillusionment and despair at what we have made of independence, but most importantly, it propounds a remedy for what he has come to see as a political impasse. *Anthills of the Savannah* also dramatises what the true role of the artist - writer, critic, carver, composer, dancer - in contemporary African societies should be: reinforcing the views expressed in "The Black Writers Burden" among his other writings. In all these, there is a discernible shift in focus in Achebe's vision and earlier concepts, and, paradoxically, in *Anthills of the Savannah* there is a synthesis and assertive projection of the views contained in the earlier works.

Achebe's latest novel highlights two basic changes in his writing. The first is the distancing of the authorial voice through the use of various narrative voices to create multiple points, while simultaneously explicating his social vision and his sense of the nature and causes of the underlying post-colonial tensions of Nigerian society. The second change is his proposition that a solution to the endemic political tensions which plague new nations of Africa is possible.

Achebe's narrative technique gives rise to such observations as Oladele Taiwo's mentioned earlier, that in Achebe's writing: "The reader finds, almost invariably, that no one point of view is wholly acceptable, and that to reach a satisfying conclusion, several points of view have to be taken into consideration" (Taiwo,p.112). Achebe presents various perspectives on the problems of contemporary African nations, represented by Kangan, through the multiple narrative voices fluctuating between the first-person point of view (Chris and Ikem), and the third-person limited point of view. It employs the self conscious narrative technique in Beatrice: "For weeks and months after I had definitely taken on the challenge of bringing together as many broken pieces of this tragic history as I could lay my hands on still I could not find a way to begin (*Anthills* p.82). But Achebe ultimately lapses into a mixture of the first person and third-person points of view manifesting an inconsistency which is in itself a measure of the complexity of the interactions of the varied perspetives. The reader as Taiwo notes, comes to the realisation that only through a synthesis of the various partial truths advocated by these individual voices could one appreciate Achebe's authorial intentions. He sees Chris' political pragmatism as an essential but partial fraction of a whole. Similarly, he recognises the corrupting influence of privilege and power which hampers Chris's awareness and development, resulting in his initial inertia and unwillingness to confront the corruption and abuse of power that he sees all around him. Achebe also views Ikem's initial idealistic reformism as a vital part of the overall political "re-form" that he advocates. Both characters' perspectives complement Beatrice's feminist activism, projecting a synthesis which, in Achebe's views, could lead to the resolution of the political tensions of these new nations.

Achebe believed that the *coup d'états* that were taking place in many African new nations were bows shooting the arrows of the gods, and that despite their being an aberration, in a vicarious way, they were necessary as the only logical resolution, at the time, for the political muddle that the Nangas have made of democracy. As he stated in the interview with Serumaga quoted earlier: "I mean the coups, themselves, are bows shooting the arrow of God. If you take the example of Nigeria, which is the place I know best, things had got to such a point politically that there was no other answer - no way you could resolve this impasse politically."[21]

In *Anthills of the Savannah* Achebe sees the soldiers as not being any better than the civilians that they ousted; if anything, they have become worse, having perfected torture, intimidation and cold-blooded killings as weapons to cow the opponents of their policies.[22] And believing that they are accountable to no one but themselves, and having the ultimate weapon - the brute force of the army at their beck and call - they have come to see governance as a matter of how long they are able to stay in or cling to power. Achebe sees the morality of good governance, principles, or the remedying of those abuses of democracy which the military saw as the reason for their intervention in the first instance, as having all been swept aside in the afterglow of power drunkenness. His Excellency sees the issues of governance in this light: "You see if Entebbe happens here it's me the world will laugh at, isn't it? Yes, it is me, General Big Mouth, they will say, and print my picture on the cover of *Time* magazine with a big mouth and a small head. . . .It's not your funeral but mine. . . .So I don't fool around. I take precautions" (*Anthills*, pp.15-6).

Therefore those who oppose his policies become "characterised as" saboteurs. Or are seen as being jealous of his person. Sam relates the personal views of the Attorney-General, that his boyhood friend, Mr Oriko, is jealous of His Excellency: "Two of you were all classmates at Lord Lugard College. He looks back to those days and sees you as the boy next door. He cannot understand how this same boy with whom he played all the boyish pranks, how he can today become this nation's Man of Destiny"(*Anthills*,.p.23) And he compares it with the views of his mentor, President-for-Life Ngongo, that: "Your greatest risk is your boyhood friends, those who grew up with you in your village. Keep them at arm's length and you will live long. The wise old tortoise!"(*Anthills*, p.23). With this comparison, His Excellency comes to see the objections of his boyhood friends,

Chris and Ikem, to some of his policies as traits of this jealousy and envy. Achebe's analysis and indictment of the educated elite that were the inheritors of power in the post-colonial era has highlighted the underlying reason for their collusion with corrupt political officials, and their own involvement with corruption. He sees both as being due to the unbridled materialism of the society; and the corrupting influence of both privilege and positions of power. Achebe's diagnosis shows that the intelligentsia has been too spineless to resist these temptations, and in *Anthills of the Savannah*, the Commissioner for Justice and Attorney-General, the Commissioner for Education, and even Mr Oriko, the Commissioner for Informationn, all exemplify this point. As Mr Oriko says of this class which includes himself:

> I am not thinking so much about him as about my colleagues, eleven intelligent, educated men who let this happen to them, who actually went out of their way to invite it, and who even at this hour have seen and learnt nothing, the cream of our society and the hope of the black race.
>
> *(Anthills, p.2)*

Achebe writes that these elite in positions of responsibility, in their debasement, would stoop to flattery, boot-licking, and back-biting in order to ingratiate themselves with those in power. Chris assaying the existing relationship between Sam and his Commissioners states that:

> On a bad day, such as this one had suddenly become after many propitious auguries, there is nothing for it but to lie close to your hole ready to scramble in. And particularly to keep your mouth shut, for nothing is safe, not even the flattery we have become such experts in disguising as debate.
>
> *(Anthills, p.3)*

He goes on to describe Professor Okong's dress which he says is aimed at impressing the military in power: "Professor Okong wears nothing but khaki safari suits complete with epaulettes. It is amazing how the intellectual envies the man of action."*(Anthills,*p.4)

But in Achebe's view, it is the Commissioner for Justice and Attorney-General that most typifies this obsequiousness:

> As for those like me, Your Excellency, poor dullards who went to bush grammar schools, we know our place, we know those better than ourselves when we see them. We have no problem worshipping a man like you. Honestly, I don't . . . .I say this, Your Excellency, to show that a man of my background has no problem

whatsoever worshipping a man like you..

(*Anthills*, p.24)

Achebe sees the boot-licking of these officials, particularly of the Commissioner for Justice and Attorney-General of a nation, as portending doom for good government. Contrary to the truth of the outcome of the referendum, that the people were blatantly manipulated, the Attorney-General curries favour by proclaiming that: "The people have spoken. Their desire is manifest. You are condemned to serve them for life "(*Anthills*, p.5). And later, having earlier told His Excellency: "My profession enjoins me to trust only hard evidence and to distrust personal feeling and mere suspicion", goes ahead to say: "I have a personal feeling . . .I don't think Chris is one hundred percent behind you . . . my impression is that he does not show any joy, any enthusiasm in matters concerning this government in general and your Excellency in particular "(*Anthills*, pp 22-3).

Through these scenes, Achebe exposes one of the *raison d'être* for the failure of most of these governments. This is the preference of those entrusted with the responsibility of advising people in power to safeguard their jobs and privileges by giving advice that they feel would be pleasing to the ears of the man in power, rather than risk his anger by giving unpalatable but necessarily honest and well-informed advice, Ikem comments that:

> The Emperor may be a fool but he isn't a monster. Not yet anyway; although he will certainly become one by the time Chris and company have done with him. . .His problem is that with so many petty interests salaaming around him all day, like that shyster of an Attorney-General, he has no chance of knowing what is right. And that's what Chris and I ought to be doing - letting him glimpse a little light now and again through chinks in his solid wall of court jesters

(*Anthills*, p.46)

Even Chris who, as Ikem says, should not compete nor fawn for His Excellency's attention, having known him longer than most, has become desensitised to the corruption and abuse of power going on around him by privilege and his closeness to power:

> Briefly our eyes had locked in combat. Then I had lowered mine to the shiny table-top in ceremonial capitulation. Long silence. But he was not appeased . . .I conceded victory there as well. Without raising my eyes I said again: "I am sorry Your Excellency." A year ago I would never have said it again that second time - without doing grave violence to myself. Now I did it like a casual favour to

him. It meant nothing at all to me - no inconvenience whatever - and everything to him.

(*Anthills*, p.1)

Rather than accuse his friend, Sam, with the facts of his misrule and if necessary, "march to the stake like a man and take the bullet in his chest", Chris tries to intellectually rationalise his own inertia and cautions Ikem on his fiery crusading editorials as "creating stupid problems for everybody. They achieve nothing. They antagonise everybody."

Achebe's criticism is that characters such as Chris and the other Commissioners, by turning courtiers and becoming "toadies in daily attendance" become caught in their new role of fawning on the powers that be, and so lose touch with the reality of the people's existence and problems. Achebe sees Chris's inertia and the general boot-licking charade of the other Commissioners as only one half of the problem, for as Ikem says, "power is like marrying across the Niger; you soon find yourself paddling by night" (*Anthills*, p.5).

The educated elite, by aligning themselves with those in power, turn a blind eye to the corruption around them, condone the abuses and excesses they see, and become themselves puppets in the hands of puppeteers. As Ikem says:

> Worshipping a dictator is such a pain in the ass. It wouldn't be so bad if it was merely a metter of dancing upside down on your head. With practice anyone could learn to do that. The real problem is having no way of knowing from one day to another, from one minute to the next, just what is up and what is down
>
> (*Anthills*, p.45)

Chris's earlier analysis sums up the corrupting influence of privilege and power, for his closeness to His Excellency had prevented him from perceiving signs of misrule and abuses that Ikem was able to interpret accurately: "I have thought of all this as a game that began innocently enough and then went suddenly strange and poisonous". But Chris could not find the specific point "at which everything went wrong and the rules were suspended" for the simple reason which he later came to realise. "And so it begins to seem to me that this thing probably never was a game, that the present was there from the beginning only I was too blind or too busy to notice" (*Anthills,*, p.2). While Achebe's summation of the cream of the society and hope of our race" is scathing, it is really on the "saviours" that he directs his satire.

Achebe's *Anthills of the Savannah* scrutinises what the military in power in the new nations of Africa, who came ostensibly to correct the political excesses and muddles of the civilian politicians, as Ascherson says, to "clear up the mess left behind by the corrupt civilian government that preceded [them]", are making of their intervention. Achebe believes that the original ideal, that of correcting the "many excesses", is still tenable but that something went awry in the execution. In his views, the change in the military leaders from crusading messiahs to corrupt military politicians was not long in eventuating. Having become exposed to the perquisite privileges of their office they were quick to change tack, to decide that remaining in power forever was better than going back to the humdrum existence of barrack life. His Excellency's excitement while narrating his experience at the OAU meeting, particularly his star-struck attitude about President-for-Life Ngongo and his bitterness at the failure of the referendum to make him one, exemplifies this fact, and belies his banter to his cabinet: "When we turn the affairs of state back to you and return to barracks that will be the time to resume your civilian tricks. Have a little more patience". Chris tells Ikem:

> But after the failure of the referendum he complained bitterly to Professor Okong that I had not played my part as Commissioner of Information to ensure the success of the exercise and that you had seen fit to abandon your editorial chair at that crucial moment and take your annual leave . . .He said that he was deeply wounded that we,his oldest friends, found it possible to abandon him and allow him to be disgraced. Those were his very words,
>
> *(Anthills,* p.147)

Achebe's astute handling of the manipulation of the referendum highlights the underlying theme, the inclination of incumbents in contemporary African nations, both civilian and military, to cling to power at whatever cost. Exploring the deviousness of this manipulation, the old man from Abazon says:

> When we were told two years ago that we should vote for the Big Chief to rule for ever and all kinds of people we had never seen before came running in and out of our village asking us to say yes I told my people: We have Osodi in Bassa. If he comes home and tells us that we should say yes we will do so because he is there as our eye and ear . . . .There was another thing that showed me there was deception in the talk. The people who were running in and out and telling us to say yes came one day and told us that the Big Chief himself did not want to rule for ever but tthat he was being

forced. Who was forcing him?
(*Anthills*, p.126)

The above recalls Chief Nanga's blatant intimidation of the people of Urua in *A Man of the People* which leads to their recanting of their support of Odili's candidacy earlier mentioned. Achebe views the use of intimidation both at the individual and the national levels as being consequent on this desire to cling to power. He sees the military rulers as having adopted the same tactics, to cow the people as the Nangas whom they ousted. The parallel with *A Man of the People* goes further, for the old man continues:

> But that was not the end. More shifting-eyes people came and said: Because you said no to the Big Chief he is very angry and has ordered all the water holes they are digging in your area to be closed so that you will know what it means to offend the sun. You will suffer so much that in you next reincarnation you will need no one to tell you to say yes whether the matter is clear to you of not.
> (*Anthills*, p.127)

Anthills of the Savannah illustrates the fact that the "soldiers-turned-politicians'have even gone futher in this wise than their civilian counterparts. By creating the secret police, they are able to stifle any oppositions and criticisms: "There were unconfirmed rumours of unrest, secret trials and executions in the barracks" (Anthills, p.14). Achebe sees these blood-lettings and the use of the secret police to brutalise and cow any dissent, as presaging a "police state". The cold-blooded killings of Ikem and Chris on two separate incidents, and the attempt to cover up the murder of Ikem, exemplify the level of degeneration of the government and its security agents. As Chris says of Ikem's death: "I am saying that there is no shred of doubt that Ikem Osodi was brutally murdered in cold blood by the security officers of this government."

In Achebe's views, the circumstances of Chris's death typify the depravity of military dictatorships to whom human life has become worthless. Achebe seems to raise the fundamental question of the humanity of a police sergeant who would attempt to rape a woman in broad daylight and in the presence of scores of witnesses, and of the society that could condone such bestiality: "She threw herself down on her buttocks in desperation. But the sergeant would not let up. He dragged her along on the seat of her once neat blue dress through clumps of scorched tares and dangers of broken glass" (*Anthills*, p.217). To Achebe, the cold blooded deliberateness of the shooting indicts not only the government that breeds such monstrosities, but the apathetic society that countenances it:

> The other said nothing more. He unslung his gun, cocked it, narrowed his eyes while confused voices went up all around some asking Chris to run, others the policeman to put the gun away. Chris stood his ground looking straight into the man's face daring him to shoot. And he did, point-blank into the chest presented to him."
>
> *(Anthills,* p.215)

Achebe's *A Man of the People* has noted the cynicism and apathy of the society. *Anthills of the Savannah* reiterates this concern. Ikem states that: "But it wasn't Authority that worried me; it never does. It was the thousands who laughed so blatantly at their own humiliation and murder." That no one of the people present raised a finger to restrain the policeman either in his attempt to rape a young school girl, excepting Chris, or stop him shooting their fellow,citizen is testimony to the degree of dehumanisation which has taken place because the society has become "sapped by [successive] regimes of parasites". That no one also, except Braimoh, makes any attempt to stop the murderer from escaping justice also illustrates the "I don't care - it is not my business" attitude of the society. Achebe writes that: "A few of the passengers, mostly other women, were pleading and protesting timorously. *But most of the men found it very funny indeed* " (*Anthills,* p.215 my italics). He believes that the brutalities perpetrated by government security agencies, from the "damnable shooting of striking railway-workers and demonstrating students" to the clamping into "solitary confinement at Bassa Maximum Security Prison" of innocent old men, have become common place occurrences, desensitising the society. Ikem sums up this insensitivity: "I knew then that if its mother was at that moment held up by her legs and torn down the middle like a piece of old rag that crowd would have yelled with eye-watering laughter."

In Achebe's view, the military leaders have also succumbed to the corruption and materialism that destroyed their civilian counterparts. Soon after ousting the civilian government for its excesses, the military leaders found it necessary to spend "twenty million" on the refurbishment of the presidential retreat built "at a cost of forty-five million", an act which Beatrice considers "irresponsibly extravagant in our circumstances". Achebe notes that while during the civilian era the politicians blatantly displayed their newly acquired wealth the military in

power resorted to the subterfuge of using front men to enrich themselves. Chris informs Beatrice that:
> Alhaji Mahmoud is himself a bit of a hermit though. He hardly appears anywhere and when he does, hardly says a word. Rumour has it that he has in the last one year knocked all other Kangan millionaires into a cocked hat. Eight ocean liners, they say, two or three private jets, a private jetty . . . . No customs officials go near his jetty and so . . he is the prince of smugglers. What else? Fifty odd companies, including a bank. Monopoly of government fertilizer imports. . . .What I find worrying and I don't think I can quite believe it yet is that (voice lowered) he may be fronting you know for . . .your host.
>
> *(Anthills*, p.117)

Achebe believes that in a society where the people's basic needs is of "water which is free from Guinea worm, of simple shelter and food", that it is the creation of such monstrous monopolies and officially sanctioned corruption that account for the perpetuation of the country's economic woes. In portraying the pervasiveness of corruption, from the Alhaji fronting for the president, to the "chaotic billing procedures deliberately done to cover their massive fraud" at the Kangan Electricity Corporation and their "readiness . . . to burn down the entire Accounts and Audit Departments if an enquiry should ever be mooted", Achebe shows that the military regime has not been able to remedy the mess or change society's attitude. Rather, they seem to have worsened the situation as exemplified by the blatant flaunting of bribery on the highways:
> Police and army checkpoints came and went fairly regularly and had dropped their pretence of looking inside the bus for the forward door. Now they took their money openly from the operators with seeming good humouron both sides. But the driver and his mate never failed to grumble and curse the fellows soon afterwards.
>
> *(Anthills, p.)*

Achebe sees the ultimate reason for the failures, chronicled in his writings, of all the succesive governments, past and present, as the failure of those in power to relate to "the very people who legitimize [their] authority". Ikem states that:
> The prime failure of this government began also to take on a clearer meaning for me. It can't be the massive corruption though its scale and pervasiveness are truly intolerable; it isn't the subservience to foreign manipulation, degrading as it is; it isn't even this second-class, hand-me-down capitalism, ludicrous and doomed; nor is it the damnable shooting of striking railway-workers and demonstrating students and the destruction and banning

thereafter of independent unions and cooperatives. It is the failure of our rulers to re-establish vital links with the poor and dispossessed of this country, with their bruised heart that throbs painfully at the core of the nation's being.

(*Anthills*, p.141)

Achebe sees this as the major failure of the civilian government, and also of the present military one. Elewa's uncle sees the issues raised in very clear and simple terms:"We have seen too much trouble in Kangan since the white man left beccause those who make plans make plans for themselves only and their families" (*Anthills*, p.228).

While *Anthills of the Savannah* affirms and even exemplifies Achebe's concept of the role of the African artist in contemporary society, it signals, however, a lateral shift in his concept of power and change. Achebe's fiction has consistently upheld the view that power, whether political or religious, derives from the people and that its possessors should be accountable to the people. Many of the excesses of such characters as Okonkwo in *Things Fall Apart,,* Ezeulu in *Arrow of God*, and Chief Nanga in *A Man of the People* derive in part from their ignoring this fact. While fundamentally this belief still underlies Achebe's latest novel, he also recalls the idea of an "enlightened dictator" being what the new nations of Africa need to put them on the right track that he first moots in *No Longer at Ease* (p.44).

However, in *Anthills of the Savannah,* Achebe raises this issue once again for scrutiny. Chris remarks of his colleagues:

> And some will add: "That's a pity because what this country really needs is a ruthless dictator. At least for five good years. And we will all laugh in loud excess because we know - bless our dear hearts - that we shall never be favoured with such and underserved blessing as a ruthless dictator.
>
> (*Anthills*,p.3)

But Achebe dismisses the idea not only because of his traditional distrust of the concentration of too much power in one individual, but mainly because he sees the wrong people as always being the ones to stumble into such positions of power; and for fear of the havoc that such individuals could wreak. As Ikem remarks about His Excellency: "If Sam were stronger or brighter he probably wouldn't need our offices; but then he probably wouldn't have become His Excellency in the first place. Only half-wits can stumble into such enormities" (*Anthills*, p.46). Through Ikem's multifaceted examination of what the notion entails, Achebe rejects it as not being the solution to the post-colonial problems of governance in contemporary Third World countries. "I wouldn't put myself under the democratic dictatorship even of angels and archangels." Ikem's exposition stresses Achebe's observation that no individual or group, in the new nations of Africa, aspire to power to use it for the benefit of the society, it is always out of self interest.

Achebe's analysis of the traditional concept and function of authority parodies the use to which power is put in contemporary African nations: "In the beginning Power rampaged through the world, naked. So the Almighty, . . . decided to send his daughter, Idemili, to bear witness to the moral nature of authority by wrapping around Power's rude waist a loincloth of peace and modesty "(*Anthills*, p.102). It is this lack of modesty, and the inability of the possessors of power to recognise the obligatory "moral nature of authority", coupled with their "unquenchable thirst to sit in authority on [their] fellows" that Idemili holds them in contempt (*Anthills*, pp.103-4).

Achebe's characterisation of His Excelllency illustrates the rapacious use of power. While the cowed attitude of the eleven civilian commissioners, in the presence of His Excellency, is indicative of the level of intimidation which they are being subjected to, Achebe, dramatises the debasing effect of "naked" power on both its wielders and their subjects, through profuse use of animal imagery. Chris narrates :

> On my right sat the Honourable Commissioner for Education. He is by far the most frightened of the lot. As soon as he had sniffed peril in the air he had begun to disappear into his hole, as some animals and insects do, backwards. Instinctively he had gathered his papers . . . dragging them into his hole after him when his entire body suddenly went rigid.
>
> (*Anthills*, p.3)

The animal imagery magnifies the impression of the "the hunter and the hunted", with the members of His Excellency's cabinet, as quarrries, always "sniffing" the air for any signs of danger, and to avoid death. But it is really in the person of Sam who became His Excellency that Achebe shows how "amazing what even one month in office can do to a man's mind" .Achebe writes that as he manipulates "his victims", His Excellency "felt again that glow of quiet jubilation that had become a frequent companion especially when as now he was disposing with consummate ease of some of those troublesome people he thought so formidable in his apprentice days in power: It takes a lion to tame a leopard, say our people. How right they are" (*Anthills*, p.22).

Achebe argues, through his analysis and accounts of the friendly relationships that have always existed between Chris, Ikem, John Kent (Mad Medico), and Sam, from their school days at Lord Lugard College, at London, and extending to Sam's early months as Head of State, that Sam is not a monster. Mad Medico sees the disintegration of this bond of friendship, and the change in Sam, as exemplifying the corrupting influence of power. He tells Dick:

> You know something, Dick, the most awful thing about power is not that it corrupts absolutely but that it makes people so utterly boring, so predictabble and . . . just plain uninteresting. . . . I told you this boy was such a charmer when I first met him. I'd never seen anyone so human, so cultured.
>
> (*Anthills*, p.56).

As a student, Chris recalls, that Sam was exemplary:

> Sam was the social paragon. . . . He was the all-rounder - good student, captain of the Cricket Team, Victor Ludorum in athletics and, in our last year, School Captain. And girls worshipped at his feet from every Girls School in the province. But strangely enough there was a kind of spiritual purity about Sam in those days despite his great weakness for girls.
>
> (*Anthills*, pp.65-6)

And later, as an officer, Ikem comments thus: "But after Sandhurst [Sam] was a catalogue model of an officer." Even after he became Head of State, in the first few months, he still retained much of his untainted personality. As Chris remarks:

> His Excellency came to power without any preparation for political leadership - a fact which he being a very intelligent person knew perfectly well . . . .Sandhurst after all did not set about training officers to take over Her Majesty's throne but rather in the high tradition of proud aloofness from politics and public affairs. Therefore when our civilian politicians finally got what they had coming to them and landed unloved and unmourned on the rubbish heap and the young Army Commander was invited by the even younger coup-makers to become His Excellency, the Head of State, he had pretty few ideas about what to do. And so, like an intelligent man, he called his friends together and said: "What shall I do?"
>
> (*Anthills*, p.12)

Achebe sees human nature as endowing individuals with the capacity both to be good and exceedingly evil. This duality, he argues, is ever present in everyone. But he believes that only one's resolve and individual circumstances determine where the balance will tilt, either to be good or bad. Ikem says that: "Man will surprise by his capacity for nobility as well as for villainy. No system can change that. It is built into the core of man's free spirit." Ikem remarks that this balance, in His Excellency's case, tilted with his first OAU meeting and his acquaintance with some military dictators from other new nations of Africa who had contrived to foist themselves on their respective nations as Presidents-for-Life. Ikem narrates that:

> I think that much of the change which has come over Sam started after his first OAU meeting. . . . He spoke like an excited schoolboy about his heroes; about the old emperor who never smiled nor changed his expression no matter what was going on around him . . . . But the leader Sam spoke most about was . . President-for-Life Ngongo, who called Sam his dear boy and invited him over to his suite for cocktails on the second day.
> (*Anthills*, pp.52-3)

Thereafter Sam also attempted, but failed, to foist himself or Kangan as President-for-Life, leading to bitterness against Ikem and Chris (for not playing their parts towards the success of the referendum), and against Abazon as the only section of the country that did not return a clear mandate: "They were the only ones whose Leaders of Thought failed to return a clear mandate to Your Excellency." Achebe's argument is that no society or system of government is good or bad. That it is the individuals who order the society or who run the government that are good or bad, because as Ikem remarks: "Society is an extension of the individual".

As already indicated, Achebe's fractured narrative technique creates multiple points of view. This not only presents the varied perspectives of the issues highlighted, it also mirrors the progression and development of the individual characters. Through shifts in time and narrative focus, the changes from first-person to third-person points of view and, as in Beatrice, to a self-conscious retrospective narrator, Achebe is able to deal more effectively with the different stages of each character's developing awareness. Achebe is thus able to circumvent the restrictions which any one single narrative technique imposes, retaining a firmer authorial control. This narrative technique is particularly important in *Anthills of the Savannah*, as it enables

Achebe to deal more overtly, and from varied perspectives, with a sensitive and contemporary post-colonial problem of some African new states misrule of gun-totting "politicians in uniform".

One of the narrators, Chris, seems to embody the fulfillment of Achebe's prediction that Odili (of *A Man of the People*) would probably return to do a better job next time. Talking to Bernth Lindfors, Achebe says of Odili:

> He was very honest. He knew his own shortcomings; he even knew when his motives were not very pure, and he admitted that these motives were not very pure. This puts him in a class worthy of attention, as far as I'm concerned. And I think he probably would return to do a better job next time . . . . But he was learning fast, and at the end I think he had improved his chances of being of service, of doing things he thought should be done. He'd improved those chances.[23]

In many ways Chris represents a more mature and perceptive Odilli. He is basically honest and acknowledges the self-interest which partly accounts for his initial inertia: "And of course, complete honesty demands that I mention one last factor in my continued stay, a fact of which I'm somewhat ashamed, namely that I couldn't be writing this if I didn't hang around to observe it all. And no one else would" (*Anthills*, p.2). He is dedicated enough to be "at work as usual long after everybody else had gone home, eaten their lunch and even had their siesta". At the outset of the narrative, Chris, as Mr Oriko, the Commissioner of Information, exemplified the corrupting influence of privilege. His lack of realistic analytical approach to social problems could justify Ikem's criticisms, that he has chosen to rationalise corruption and Sam's progressive irrationalities because of his position (*Anthills*, p.38). As Beatrice and Ikem remarked on his failure to see beyond His Excellency,s comments about their roles in the failure of the referendum: "It doesn't speak too highly of your power of analysis or insight which is what I have always told you." It took Ikem's brutal murder to galvanise Chris from his political pragmatism and animal sense of self-preservation, towards more courageous action. Achebe implies criticism by Beatrice's use of the term "reasonableness" when she cautions herself: "Careful now before you find yourself slowly and secretly leaning towards Chris's reasonableness!"(*Anthills*,p.73). But by the end Chris was willing, even at the risk of his own life, to do "the things he thought should be done" such as protecting innocent civilians from the excesses of gun-totting men in uniform.

However, it is through Ikem Osodi that Achebe explores and explicates many of the theories and abstractions that his earlier writings, prose fiction, poetry and essays, have sought to define - of the true role of the artist in contemporary African societies which, he believes, is that they should have vision, criticise injustices in their societies, and through their vision and criticism, direct their society in the path that it should be heading. Nadine Gordimer rightly observes in her review of *Anthills of the Savannah* that "even a defence of the role of the writer as opposed to the demand that he become a revolutionary - or a reformist-activist in relation to his people comes naturally, not authorially, from the mouth of an old Abazon storyteller"[24]. Achebe dramatises the writer's function, through the old man's analysis, and Ikem embodies this concept. Nadine Gordimer quoting Achebe, writes:

> 'We all imagine that the story of the land is easy, that everyone of us can get up and tell it.' But the writer is the one whose eye the gods have 'ringed . . . with white chalk . . . .He may be a fellow of little account, not the bold warrior we all expect not even the war drummer. But in his new-found utterance our struggle will stand reincarnated before us. He is the liar who can sit under his thatch and see the moon hanging in the sky outside. Without stirring from his stool he can tell you how commodities are selling in a distant market place. His chalked eye will see every blow in a battle he never fought.'[25]

Achebe sees the writer [press] as representing in the final analysis, the conscience of the society; and should uphold and protect whatever fundamental principles on which that society is built. Ikem sustains Achebe's advocacy that "one of the writer's main functions has always been to expose and attack injustice"[26]. And that: "We must seek the freedom to express our thought and feeling even against ourselves, without the anxiety that what we say might be taken in evidence against our race".[27]

Ikem is shown to be willing to undergo deprivation rather than forsake his principles. To Chris's exhortation for "editorial restraint" Ikem replies: "As for my editorials, as long as I remain editor of the *Gazette* I shall not seek anybody's permission for what I write . . . .If you don't like it you know what to do, Chris, don't you? You hired me, didn't you?" (*Anthills*, p.44). Chris admits that the mere notion of "editorial restraint" outrages Ikem:

> That's why I have said a hundred million times to Ikem; Lie low

for a while and this gathering tornado may rage and pass overhead carrying away roof-tops and perhaps . . . only perhaps . . . leave us battered but alive. But oh no! Ikem is outraged that I should recommend such cowardly and totally unworthy behaviour to him (Anthills,.p.119)

Achebe believes that the responsibility that artists bear is such that their justification at all times for what they do should be what is best for the society, not whether those in authority agree to their views, not even whether the views antagonise or create problems for everyone as Chris argues. Nor should it be based on its futility. "But supposing my crusading editorials were indeed futile would I not be obliged to keep on writing them?"(*Anthills*, p.38).

Again Chris argues that Ikem lacks political pragmatism, that he is "a romantic; and . . . had no solid contact with the ordinary people of Kangan." He further claims that Ikem is an "artist who has the example of Don Quixote and other fictional characters to guide him"(*Anthills*, p.119). Three separate incidents would suffice to illustrate not only Achebe's answer to this charge, but more importantly, they will exemplify how well Ikem lives up to the role which Achebe believes that he and his class should be performing. The incident of the public execution of armed robbers and Ikem's editorial "calling on the President to promulgate forthwith a decree abrogating the law that permitted that outrageous and revolting performance". leads to the promulgation of the Public Executions Amendment Decree (although Chris denies this), and testify to the efficacy of editorials. But, it is probably the comments of the two taxi drivers, and from the old man of Abazon that fully illustrate the points that Achebe makes through Ikem.

The two taxi drivers' visit illustrates that society's awareness of the functioning of good and responsible press. One of the men, though uneducated, yet showed a marked appreciation of the effectiveness of Ikem's editorials which Ikem found illuminating: "But na for we small people he de write every time. I no sabi book but I sabi say na for we this oga de fight, not for himself. He na big man. Nobody fit do fuckall to him. So he fit stay for him house, chop him chop, drink him cold beer, put him air conditioner and foget we, But he no do like that. So we come salute am "(Anthills,.p.136). His friend's analysis of the remedial outcome of Ikem's editorial on the stinking "Central Taxi Park for Slaughter Road", clearly shows that Ikem "is in touch with the ordinary people" of Kangan, that he articulates

some of the society's aspirations, and that the society appreciates what he is doing.
But Achebe's most important illustration of the effectiveness of Ikem's editorials is given by the old man from Abazon. Overwhelmed by the campaign from those who wanted to influence their decision, to force them to acquiesce in the Head of State becoming Life-President, the people of Abazon decided to wait on "the bastion of democracy".[28] Their reasoning was that the type of writers represented by Ikem were their eyes and ears. That in this capacity, they would see and responsibly evaluate the pros and cons of the issues at stake. That thereafter, if Ikem asks them to acquiesce in the demand, either by coming personally or writing in his editorials, they would "But he did not come to tell us and he did not write in his paper. So we knew that cunning had entered the talk" (*Anthills*, p.131). The old man, like most members of the society, and one of the taxi drivers is uneducated, yet appreciative of the value of Ikem's editorials: "I have never read what they say he writes because I do not know ABC. But I have heard of all the fight he has fought for poor people in this land" (*Anthills*, pp.122-3). That the society could come to depend on the Press for guidance, on an issue of national significance, is testimony that the Press was doing one of its jobs - enlightenment: "I have shown what light I can with a number of controversial editorials".

Through Ikem's reformist analysis of power, societal ills, and vision for the future, one appreciates Achebe's modified proposal for the resolution of some of the post-colonial tensions of the society. Achebe believes that the solution to the perennial problems of constant changes of government and blood-letting, cannot be in the systems of governments, whatever they are. Ikem states that the various "simplistic remedies touted by all manner of salesmen . . . will always fail because of man's stubborn antibody called surprise". In Achebe's views, the "reformism", whether "bourgeois" or "democratic dictatorship of the proletariat" that many of these new nations of Africa advocate, is doomed to failure. This, Achebe says, is because any manner of reform could only be meaningful and viable if it is built around society's existing core of values. To change the system totally, he says, portends disaster. Ikem analyses and projects this view saying::

> The most we can hope to do with a problematic individual psyche is to reform it. No responsible psychoanalyst would aim to do

more, for to do more, to overthrow the psyche itself, would be to unleash insanity. No. We can only hope to rearrange some details in the periphery of the human personality. Any disturbance of its core is an irresponsible invitation to disaster . . . . .It has to be the same with society. You re-form it around what it is, its core of reality; not around an intellectual abstraction."

(*Anthills*, pp.99-100)

Achebe sees this mode of reform as the "most promising" solution. "Reform may be a dirty word then but it begins to look more and more like the most promising route to success in the real world." Both Ikem's advocacy for "re-form" and his departure from his earlier arrogant male-dominance are expressions of a new awareness. And a manifestation of his rejection of a hitherto held radical marxism; recognising the viability of other forms of governance, but more importantly, the fact that the "problem" is with the people - the governed and the governors - and not with the system. His speech to the students is the culmination of his political development which has progressively become more pronounced as the extent of government excesses became apparent.

Starting with his fiery editorials, through his feminist discourse with Beatrice, and further expounded in his speech to the students, Ikem highlights the malaise of the polity; but he believes that no meaningful political progress could be made without including mass participation of the people - taxi drivers, market women, students and labourers. For, these are "the very people that legitimize" the existence of any government. Ikem's speech to the students puts all classes of people into a political balance, and finds them wanting, but his faith in the future transcends this immediate failing. His public proclamation of his intent to marry an "ordinary illiterate" petty-trader's daughter, like his preference for his old and battered car (to being chauffeur-driven in a company car), pledges his faith in a society not governed by class and status. It is this faith that galvanises, not only his friend Chris, but also the student leaders to see beyond his death to his vision of a tomorrow, in which "power" is used rightly for the benefit of society. A vision which only began to dawn on Chris at his last moments: "Chris was sending us a message to beware. This world belongs to the people of the world not to any little caucus, no matter how talented" (*Anthills*, p.232). Elewa's child symbolises this faith and vision, not only as the living proof of a union that cuts across social barriers but, as Elewa's uncle and the whole assembly acquiesced, "the daughter of all of us".

But his most profound advocacy, which is also built around the premise of society's existent inherent reality, is the invocation (and modification) of the female principle:

> But the way I see it is that giviing women today the same role which traditional society gave them of intervening only when everything else has failed is not enough, you know, like the women in the Sembene film who pick up the spears abandoned by their defeated menfolk. It is not enough that women should be the court of last resort because the last resort is a damn sight too far and too late!!

(*Anthills*, pp.91-2)

Beatrice's function is not only as a narrative voice, articulating and projecting Achebe's new vision of the role of women in the "days ahead", but she serves to moderate between the views of Chris and Ikem, and more importantly, to sharpen and focus Ikem's, and consequently. Achebe's proffered solution. Ikem's development from (as Chris believes) a romantic idealist towards a more practical reformism, and a less male arrogance, recognising that women have a new role to play in the times ahead, complements and heightens Beatrice's political perception. Ikem claims that he owes his insight on the feminist concept to Beatrice. He argues that from antiquity Man had chauvinistically assigned to women, the role of the world's "fire-brigade after the house has caught fire and been virtually consumed" (*Anthills*, p.97). That through the ages, from the times of the Old Testament to the present, of the New Testament, Man has striven to relegate the female principle to a degree of irrelevancy:

> So the idea came to Man to turn his spouse into the very Mother of God, to pick her up from right under his feet where she'd been since Creation and carry her reverently to a nice, corner pedestal. Up there, her feet completely off the ground she will be just as irrelevant to the practical decisions of running the world as she was in her bad old days. The only difference is that now Man will suffer no guilt feelings; he can sit back and congratulate himself on his generosity and gentlemanliness.

(*Anthills*, p.98)

Achebe believes that the time is now, for the new nations of Africa, to invoke the female principle, not necessarily in its original form of keeping women "in reserve until the ultimate crisis arrives and the waist is broken and hung over the fire, and the palm bears the fruit at the tail of its leaf. Then, as the world crashes around Man's ears, Woman in her supremacy will descend and sweep the shards together" (*Anthills*, p.98). But in response to Beatrice's question: "What must a people do to appease an embittered history?" Ikem's visionary answer, which Beatrice echoes, is that: "It is now up to you women to tell us what has to be done." Achebe also uses Beatrice to synthesise both Ikem's and Chris's dialectics and views about the nature of society, and consequently project his own - that the society belongs to everyone and that those vested with authority exercise such on behalf of that society. Beatrice sums up these views thus: "This world belongs to the people of the world not to any little caucus, no matter how talented."

Anthills of the Savannah finally advocates, in conjunction with the incorporation of the female principle, a system of government whose foundation would be laid on a deep appreciation of the ethnic and religious diversities of the new nations of Africa: "Well, if a daughter of Allah could join his rival's daughter in a holy dance, what is to stop the priestess of the unknown god from shaking a leg?" (*Anthills*, p.224). But it is Elewa's uncle that sums this view in his prayer for the new born baby:

> 'But we have no quarrel with church people; we have no quarrel with mosque people. Their intentions are good, their mind on the right road. Only the hand fails to throw as straight as the eye sees. We praise a man when he slaughters a fowl so that if his hand becomes stronger tomorrow he will slaughter a goat. . . May this child be the daughter of all of us. . . May these young people here when they make the plans for the world not forget her. And all other children.'
>
> (*Anthills*, p.228)

Elewa's uncle's prayer provides an appropriate opening for concluding this chapter, in that its condensed aphorisms highlight some of the major flaws which Achebe's writings have shown as being primarily responsible for the post-colonial tensions of the Nigerian state. His appreciation of the inherent good in opposed religions as Islam and Christianity embodies Achebe's belief in non-sectarianism in policies of national significance. But, as has happened with the political legacy, "only the hand fails to throw as straight as the eye sees". *Anthills of the Savannah* has shown that, as with their civilian counterparts the intentions of military when they assumed office were good, but something went awry in the execution. The prayer that, "those in whose hands it is to plan their world" should not forget the new-born child, and all other children, reiterates Achebe's concern with the tendency of people in power to forget the people they govern. But while Achebe's recent fiction proffers such solutions as "wrapping around power's rude waist a loincloth of peace and modesty" and using power with responsibility, he advocates above all, that leaders of Africa's new nations, particularly Nigeria, should take into full consideration the needs and aspirations of their varied members.

CONCLUSION

When one considers that Achebe writes from a society that is totally indigenous, because the colonialists left after his society became independent, the depth of his social vision assumes great significance. Of particular relevance are his views on the role of the imaginative writer in contemporary society. Achebe com ments in his essay, "The Novelist as Teacher", in which he relates the story of the boy in his wife's class, quoted earlier. "I think it is part of my business as a writer to teach that boy that there is nothing disgraceful about the African weather, that the palm-tree is a fit subject for poetry."[1] Considered alongside his often quoted statement: "I would be quite satisfied if my novels (especially the ones I set in the past) did no more than teach my readers that their past - with all its imperfections - was not one long night of savagery from which the first Europeans acting on God's behalf delivered them,"[2] Achebe's social and political consciousness preludes the condoning of lapses which verge on squandering of both traditional and inherited political legacies, as is prevalent among the black nations of Africa As a writer Achebe has had to recreate his society's historical pasts to counter earlier assumptions that the indigenous peoples did not have any history or culture. Achebe believes that the validating of his people's past which his early writings represented, was a form of protest:

> I believe that it is impossible to write anything in Africa without some kind of commitment, some kind of message, some kind of protest. Even those early·novels . . . what they were saying, in effect, was that we had a past. That was protest, because there were people who thought we didn't have a past. . . . The whole pattern of life demanded that . . . you should put in a word for your history, your traditions, your religion, and so on.[3]

But while in the early periods of his development, Achebe assiduously cultivated and developed themes that highlighted the indigenous cultures and traditions of the respective societies that are depicted in his writings, both for the enlightenment of his own culturally alienated people, as he says, and also the larger society, his later writings have shown shifts of emphasis. Achebe's recent writings show a marked sense of disillusionment at the mess that the emergent African administrative class, and by extension the self-governing countries of Africa, have made of self-rule. Achebe's *hiatus*, which was partly forced on him by circumstances over which he had no control, has nevertheless, affected his vision and social consciousness as a writer. This *hiatus* engendered a more intense sense of disillusionment, and of betrayal for, as Philip Rogers notes in his analysis of Achebe's poem, "Lazarus", in which Ogbaku people kill their kinsman "on the threshold of a promising resurrection", "the moment of birth is blighted, but the blighting force can no longer be dismissed as external"[4]. This is a summation of Achebe's despair at what his people have become, or more appropriately, done with their inheritance. But more importantly, the *hiatus* has renewed, in Achebe, a determination to criticise the failings of those entrusted with the destinies of the new states of Africa as evidenced by his latest novel, *Anthills of the Savannah*.

It is apparent from this study that Achebe believes that his proposals for the resolution of his society's post-colonial tensions to be the most efficacious for the society. Many critics of Achebe's post-war writings - Kolawole Ogungbesan, David Carroll, and Philip Rogers, among others - have noted his quest for the place of the modern artist.[5] They have also identified his sense of the writer as being an unwanted seer in contemporary, often militarily-ruled, nations of Africa. His *Anthills of the Savannah* attests to the end of the search, as he tells Kim Heron: "This horrendous experience [the Nigerian civil-war] was, for me, the end of an epoch, and it really drew a curtain across modern African history . . . I needed to sit back and reflect before saying anything more."[6] While in *No Longer at Ease* Achebe, even as he uses a character such as Mr Green to highlight some of the failings of the emergent black administrative class, also holds "the Greens" partly culpable for "the Obis", who were "half-baked" products of partial socialisation; *A Man of the People* and now, *Anthills of the Savannah* dump most of the blames at the door-steps of Africans (and other indigenous people) themselves. Achebe's often quoted proverb, that "the man who brings ant-infested faggots into the hut should not grumble when lizards begin to pay him a visit", assumes relevance when juxtaposed with his criticism of what the indigenous peoples of Africa are making of their political inheritance. This is probably most exemplified by Ngugi Wa Thiong'o's analysis of *A Man of the People* which aptly applies equally to *Anthills of the Savannah*. Having established in his analysis that "the leaders of the anti-colonial struggle have become traitors to their peoples' cause and have sacrificed Africa on the alter of their own middle-class comfort"[7], Ngugi goes on to say that Achebe in *A Man of the People,*

> . . . .has turned his back on the European presence. He no longer feels the need to explain, or point out mistakes, by merely recreating . . . . Now, in *A Man of the People* and *Anthills of the Savannah*, the teacher talks to his pupils, directly. He has lost patience. He retains self-control in that he does not let anger drive him into incoherent rage and wild lashing. Instead he takes his satirical whip and raps his pupils - with rage, of course, sometimes with pathos verging on tears, but often with bitterness, though this is hardly discernible because below it flow compassion and a zest for life.[8]

Ngugi particularly notes that in these writings, "the teacher accuses them all of complicity in the corruption that has beset our society. Your indifference and cynicism has given birth to and nurtured Chief Nanga [Sam, and others like them]," he says. Continuing, he says. "The teacher no longer stands apart to contemplate. He has moved with a whip among the pupils, flagellating himself as well as them", and as has been noted in the course of this study, he makes the point that: "What Achebe has done in [both] *A Man of the People [and Anthills of the Savannah]* is to make it impossible or inexcusable for other African writers to do other than address themselves directly to their audiences in Africa . . . and tell them that such problems are their concern."[9]

Despite the historical impact of colonialsim on the indigenous peoples of Africa, particularly Nigeria, Achebe's writings, their social realism and understanding of the dialectics of social change, coupled with the fact that in such countries as Nigeria the colonialists left after independence, presupposes that the administrators of these states are culpable. Arguably these writings demonstrate that there is no universal solution to postcolonial tensions, nevertheless, irrespective of their origin and nature their message is clear: the present generation of the indigenous people, particularly African black nations, have a salvaging job of paramount importance to them and posterity - to salvage what is useful from their past, graft those to what is useful from European culture, and re-form the colonial political and social heritage around their existing cultural world-view - if the present generation is to avoid the cultural dislocation that will eternally condemn them, and the future generations to perpetual underdevelopment.

NOTES

Introduction

[1] In view of the complex multiplicity of ethnic groups in Nigeria the use of Ibo, within the context of Achebe's analysis of societal malaise, becomes representative. Further more, it will be used interchangeably with Igbo. This usage acknowledges the fact that while Igbo language purists would insist on Ibo being used to distinguish the people and Igbo, the language, most contemporary writers now use Ibo to represent both the people and the language, while Igbo still represents only the language. However, in the Igbo-speaking rural areas the reverse is the case as most people use Igbo alone to represent both the people and the language.

[2] As with most "all-embracing" terms "Commonwealth" generates considerable debate among critics as to its suitability. Some have opted for such other classifications as "Third World Literature", "Literatures written in either English or French" but Commonwealth is used here, for want of a better term, much as Ferres and Tucker, among others, argue for and use it in the introduction to their Modern Commonwealth Literature as the most practical term which could include such diverse writers as Wole Soyinka and Chinua Achebe alongside Witi Ihimaera and Albert Wendt or George Lamming.

[3] Chinua Achebe, "Interview by Robert Serumaga," *African Writers Talking*, eds, Dennis Duerden and Cosmo Pieterse, (London: Heinemann, 1972), p. 13.

[4] Witi Ihimaera, "The Maori Affairs Syndrome," Editorial, *New Zealand Listener*, (Aug. 27, 1977), p.10.

[5] Roy Murphy, "A Boy from Gisborne Pens a Success Story in the Big Apple: Reluctant Writer Comes of Age," The Dominion Sunday Times, (Jun. 7, 1987), p. 13.

[6] Another Nigerian writer, Wole Soyinka, in an interview with Biodun Jeyifo in 1983 also indicts this first batch of administrative class, particularly legislators, saying: "I took one look at our first set of legislators . . . when they visited the UK and talked to students, I listened to them, watched them, and I knew . . . That instant, I think I received what the Japanese might term *political satori* you know, instant illumination. I realised that the first enemy was within." Biodun Jeyifo, Introduction: based on "Interview with Wole Soyinka," *Six Plays* by Wole Soyinka, (London: Methuen, 1984), p. xiii.

[7] Ime Ikiddeh, Foreword, *Homecoming: Essays on African and Caribbean Literature, Culture and Politics*, by Ngugi Wa Thiong'o, (London: Heinemann, 1972), pp. xi-xii.

[8] Chinua Achebe, "The Role of the Writer in a New Nation," *African Writers on African Writing*, ed, G.D.Killam, (Evanston: Northwestern University Press, 1973), p. 11.

[9] This phrase is most often used to include both the colonised and coloniser, but Achebe's interest is primarily with what the African's themselves are making of their inheritance.

Chapter One

[1] Chinua Achebe, "Named for Victoria, Queen of England," *Morning Yet on Creation Day*, (London: Heinemann, 1975), p. 70.

[2] Nkosi Lewis, "Interview with Chinua Achebe in Lagos, August 1962," *African Writers Talking*, Ed. by Dennis Duerden and Cosmo Pieterse. (London: Heinemann,1972), p. 4.

[3] Nkosi Lewis, p. 5.

[4] Philip Rogers, "Chinua Achebe's Poems of Regeneration," *Journal of Commonwealth Literature* , 10.3 (1976): p.1.

[5] Arthur Ravenscroft, *Chinua Achebe*, (London: Longmans, Green and Co., 1969), p. 7.

[6] Chinua Achebe, "The Role of the Writer in a New Nation," *African Writers on African Writing*, Ed.G.D.Killam, Evanston: Northwestern Univ. Press, 1973), p.9.

[7] P.Cairns, "Style, Structure and the Status of Language in Chinua Achebe's *Things Fall Apart* and *Arrow Of God*," *World Literature Written in English*, 25.1 (1985), pp. 1-9.

[8] Philip Rogers, p.1.

[9] Kofi Awoonor, *The Breast of the Earth*, (New York: Anchor Press, 1976), p. 252.

[10] Chinua Achebe, "The Role of the Writer in a New Nation," *African Writers on African Writing*, pp. 7-8.

[11] Chinua Achebe, "The Role of the Writer in a New Nation," *African Writers on African Writing*, p. 8.

[12] Chukwudi T. Maduka, "The African Writer and the Drama of Social Change," Ariel, 12.3 (1981), p. 11.

[13] Chinua Achebe, "The Black Writer's Burden," Présence Africaine (Paris), 31 (1966), p.139.

[14] Adrian Roscoe, Mother is Gold: A Study in West African Literature, (Cambridge: Cambridge University Press, 1971), p.122.

[15] Wilfred Cartey, *Whispers from a Continent: the Literature of Contemporary Black Africa*, (London: Heinemann, 1971), p. 160.

[16] David Murphy, *The Silent Watchdog: the Press in Local Politics*, (London: Constable, 1976), p. 11.

[17] René Wellek, *Concepts of Criticism*, (New Haven, 1963), pp. 238-9.

[18] Bernth Lindfors et al, eds, *Palaver: Interviews with Five African Writers*, (Austin,Texas: African and Afro-American Research Institute, 1972), pp.11-12.

[19] Bernth Lindfors et al, eds, *Palaver: Interviews with Five African Writers*, (Austin,Texas: African and Afro-American Research Institute, 1972) p. 6.

[20] Bernth Lindfors et al, eds, *Palaver: Interviews with Five African Writers*, (Austin,Texas: African and Afro-American Research Institute, 1972), p. 8.

[21] Chinua Achebe's essay, "Colonialist Criticism", is based on a paper read to the Association for Commonwealth Literature and Language Studies at Makerere University, Uganda, in January 1974; it is included in both Killam's *African Writers on African Writing* and in Achebe's book of essays, *Morning Yet on Creation Day*, pp. 10-11.

[22] Neal Ascherson, "Betrayal," New York Review of Books 35.3 (Mar. 3, 1988), pp.3-6. "Some of the points which Neal Ascherson's review makes of Achebe and his writing, particularly his stress on the issue of lack of responsibility, I have already arrived at independently. Also Nadine Gordimer's review harps on this issue of individual responsibility:'The ethos of this book is individual responsibility, and, whatever one's experience on the individual's limited effectiveness in the struggle for justice may have been, this ethos is presented with overwhelming conviction.'"A Tyranny of Clowns," *The New York Times Book Review* (Feb. 21, 1988), pp. 1, 26.

Chapter Two

[1] Chinua Achebe, "The Role of the Writer in a New Nation," *African Writers on African Writing*, ed G. D. Killam, p.10.

[2] Chinua Achebe, "The Role of the Writer in a New Nation," *African Writers on African Writing*, ed G. D. Killam, p. 14.

[3] In Igbo culture it is taboo in most places for people of the same village to intermarry because of the descent pattern from which villages are derived. Most families within a village trace their origins to the same ancestor, hence most public addresses begin with the greetings: "Umunnem na Umunnam" meaning fellow descendants from the same ancestral mother and father.

[4] Chinua Achebe, "The Role of the Writer in a New Nation," *African Writers on African Writing*, p.9.

[5] David Carroll, *Chinua Achebe*, (New York: St. Martin's Press, 1980), p. 16.

[6] Arthur Ravenscroft, *Chinua Achebe*, (London: Longman, Green and Co., 1969), p. 16.

[7] Neil McEwan, *Africa and the Novel*, (London: Macmillan, 1983), p. 21.

[8] Oladele Taiwo, *Culture and the Nigerian Novel*, (New York: St. Martin's Press, 1976), p. 112

[9] Eustace Palmer does not share this view. He notes in *An Introduction to th African Novel* that Achebe "does not merely record these instances of savagery without implying any judgement, for he carefully leaves clues and hints, structural as well as textual, as comments on the nature of the society he describes. pp. 52-3.

[10] G.D.Killam, "Notions of Religion, Alienation and Archetype in *Arrow of God*," *Exile and Tradition*, ed Rowland Smith, (New York: Africana Publishing Company,1976),

[11] G.D.Killam, *The Novels of Chinua Achebe*, (London: Heinemann, 1969), p. 16.

[12] Eustace Palmer, *An Introduction to the African Novel*, (London: Heinemann, 1972), p. 53.

[13] Arthur Ravenscroft, *Chinua Achebe*, p.13.

[14] Critics have Soyinka as supposedly having said that: "I don't think a tiger has to go around proclaiming his tigritude", which Soyinka corrected in a recording taped by Janheinz Jahn in 1964, because it was taken out of context and says: I said "A tiger does not proclaim his tigritude, he pounces .... When you pass where the tiger has walked before, you see the skeleton of the duiker, you know that some tigritude has been emanated there." For context and more details see Hans M. Zell, and Helene Silver, comps and eds, "Wole Soyinka," *A Reader's Guide to African Literature* (London: Heinemann, 1972), pp. 191-2.

[15] Chinua Achebe, *Things Fall Apart*, pp. 7, 24-5.

[16] Chinua Achebe, "The Role of the Writer in a New Nation," *African Writers on African Writing*, p. 11.

[17] Chinua Achebe, "The Role of the Writer in a New Nation," *African Writers on African Writing*, p. 11.

[18] Chinua Achebe, "Interview by Robert Serumaga," *African Writers Talking*, eds, Dennis Duerden and Cosmo Pieterse, (London: Heinemann, 1972), p. 14.

[19] Chinua Achebe, "Interview by Robert Serumaga," *African Writers Talking*, eds, Dennis Duerden and Cosmo Pieterse, (London: Heinemann, 1972), p. 16.

[20] Chinua Achebe, "Interview by Robert Serumaga," *African Writers Talking*, eds, Dennis Duerden and Cosmo Pieterse, (London: Heinemann, 1972), p. 16.

[21] Chinua Achebe, "Interview by Lewis Nkosi," African Report (July 1964), p. 20. Quoted by G.D. Killam in *The Novels of Chinua Achebe*, p. 60.

[22] Chinua Achebe, "Interview by Lewis Nkosi," African Report (July 1964), p. 20. Quoted by G.D. Killam in *The Novels of Chinua Achebe*, p. 9.

[23] This has been highlighted by David Carroll's comments about Igbo traditional society's attitude to change and the individual, mentioned in relation to Okonkwo, but it is unequivocally illustrated in Achebe's analysis of power in *Anthills of the Savannah* which will be discussed later in this section.

[24] Chinua Achebe, "Interview by Robert Serumaga," *African Writers Talking*, p. 9.

[25] Chinua Achebe, "Preface to Second Edition," *Arrow of God*.

Chapter Three

[1] Gerald Moore, *Seven African Writers*, (London: Oxford University Press, 1962), p. 59.

[2] Bernth Lindfors, et al., eds, "Interview with Chinua Achebe," *Palaver: Interviews with Five African Writers in Texas*, (Austin, Texas: African and Afro-American Research Institute, 1972), p. 12.

[3] Chinua Achebe, "Interview by Robert Serumaga," *African Writers Talking*, p. 13.

[4] G.D. Killam, "Notions of Religion, Alienation and Archetype in *Arrow of God*," *Exile and Tradition* ed. by Rowland Smith. (New York: Africana Publishing Company, 1976), p. 154.

[5] Chinua Achebe, "The Role of the Writer in a New Nation," *African Writers on African Writing*, p. 10.

[6] Chinua Achebe, "The Role of the Writer in a New Nation," *African Writers on African Writing*, pp. 10-11.

[7] Neal Ascherson, "Betrayal," Rev. of *Anthills of the Savannah* by Chinua Achebe, New York Review of Books, 35.3 (Mar. 3, 1988), p. 3.

[8] Shantto Arthur Gakwandi, *The Novel and Contemporary Experience in Africa*, (New York: Africana Publishing Company, 1977), p.27.

[9] John Povey, "The Novels of Chinua Achebe," *Introducation to Nigerian Literature*, ed, Bruce King, (New York: Africana Pub. Corp.1971), p.105.

[10] Achebe develops this theme further in his essay "The African Writer and the Biafran Cause", published in his book of essays, *Morning Yet on Creation Day*.

[11] Chinua Achebe, *No Longer at Ease*, pp. 61, 69, 89,95, 99, 100, 125. "Steward's actual salary is not indicated, but given the status consciousness of the society, and that salary differences are normal ways of emphasising this status, it could not be less than the amount stated here when compared to the gardener's salary of 10.6 x 6 flats = 3.3 monthly.

[12] Garri is a Nigerian staple food.

[13] "Been to" is a Nigerian euphemism in the 1950's and 1960's for Nigerians who have travelled overseas, particularly to Europe.

[14] Chinua Achebe, *The Trouble with Nigeria*, (London: Heinemann, 1984), (first published by Fourth Dimension Publishing Co., Nigeria, 1983), p. 1.

[15] Chinua Achebe, *No Longer at Ease*, pp.104-5. (Note Mr Green's comments on the issue of yearly car insurance which questions Obi's level of responsibility. Surely, anyone who buys a car should be aware that periodically he would be expected to renew the person's car and driver's licences, and the car's insurance policy on expiry. But Obi proves this assumption wrong as evidence shows: when his insurance policy expires he was not prepared. Also note Obi's naivety as analysed by Ravenscroft in relation to the issue of income tax which will be looked into later.)

[16] David Cook, *African Literature*, (London: Longman Group, 1977), p. 91.

[17] Chinua Achebe, "Named for Victoria, Queen of England," *Morning Yet on Creation Day*, p. 68.

[18] Adrian A. Roscoe, *Mother is Gold: A Study in West African Literature*, (Cambridge, England: Cambridge University Press, 1971), p.125.

[19] Wilfred Cartey, *Whispers from the Continent*, (London: Heinemann, 1971), p.176.

[20] The analysis of the Osu *caste system* shows that Igbo elders regard it as evil and Obi's father exemplifies how objectionable most parents find such liaisons.

[21] Chinua Achebe, "Interview by Robert Serumaga," *African Writers Talking*, p. 13.

[22] Chinua Achebe, "Interview by Robert Serumaga," *African Writers Talking*, p. 13.

[23] Neal Ascherson, "Betrayal," Rev. of *Anthills of the Savannah* by Chinua Achebe, New York Review of Books, 35.3 (Mar. 3, 1988), p. 3.

[24] Neal Ascherson, "Betrayal," Rev. of *Anthills of the Savannah* by Chinua Achebe, New York Review of Books, 35.3 (Mar. 3, 1988), p. 3.

[25] Wole Soyinka, "The Writer in a Modern African State," *The Writer in Modern Africa*, ed. by Per Wastberg, (New York: Africana Publishing Corporation, 1969), p. 21.

[26] Eldred Jones, "Locale and Universe -Three Nigerian Novels," *Journal of Commonwealth Literature* 3 (Jul. 1967), p. 130.

[27] The proverb is used in contemporary African societies to support the unscrupulous use of "the power of incumbency". Chief Nanga's flaunting of 'power' gives rise to the belief that since he holds the power, and with it the people's welfare, he has a right to dictate to the people how they are to be governed, and who they should cast their vote for.

[28] David Carroll, *Chinua Achebe*, p. 127.
[29] Michael Neill, "Coming Home: Teaching the Post-Colonial Novel," *Islands* 2 (1985), p.49.
[30] Chinua Achebe, "Interview by Robert Serumaga," *African Writers Talking*, pp. 13-4.
[31] Eustace Palmer, *An Introduction to the African Novel*, (London: Heinemann, 1972), p. 73.
[32] Chinua Achebe, "Chinua Achebe talking to Tony Hall," Sunday Nation (Nairobi), 15 Jan. 1967, p. 15. Quoted from *A reader's Guide to African Literature*, eds, Hans Zell and Helene Silver, (London: Heinemann, 1972), pp. 118-9.
[33] Ngugi Wa Thiong'o, "The Writer in a Changing Society," *Homecoming: Essays on African and Caribbean Literature, Culture and Politics*, (London: Heinemann, 1972), p. 54.
[34] Ngugi Wa Thiong'o, "The Writer in a Changing Society," *Homecoming: Essays on African and Caribbean Literature, Culture and Politics*, (London: Heinemann, 1972), p. 54.
[35] Bernth Lindfors, et al., eds, *Palaver: Interviews with Five African Writers*, p. 12.

Chapter Four

[1] Chinua Achebe, "Interview by Robert Serumaga," *African Writers Talking*, p. 14.
[2] Chinua Achebe, "Interview by Robert Serumaga," *African Writers Talking*., p. 14.
[3] Bernth Lindfors, et al., p.11.
[4] Bernth Lindfors, et al., p. 5.
[5] Bernth Lindfors, et al., p. 6.
[6] Some Nigerian writers and critics, amongst them, J. P. Cark (see Bernth Lindfors, et al., *Palaver: Interviews with Five African Writers in Texas*, pp. 15-22), and Kolawole Ogungbesan, (see "Politics and the African Writer," *African Studies Review* 17 (1974), pp. 43-53), have been very critical of Achebe and other Igbo creative writers, particularly Christopher Okigbo, and claim that they prostituted their vocation as writers by being actively involved in the war, and Achebe for writing so realistically about the experience. Consequently, Ogungbesan, among others, see no literary merit in Achebe's writings of this period.
[7] Chinua Achebe, "Where the Problem Lies," *The Trouble with Nigeria*, (First published by Fourth Dimension Publishing Co., Enugu, Nigeria in 1983. London: Heinemann, 1984), p. 2.
[8] Chinua Achebe, "Girls at War," *Girls at War and Other Stories*, (London: Heinemann, 1972), p. 114.

9 Arthur Ravenscroft, "The Nigerian Civil War in Nigerian Literature," *Commonwealth Literature and the Modern World*, ed. Hena Maes-Jelinek (Bruxelles: Libraire Marcel Didier, 1975), p.108.

10 Arthur Ravenscroft, "The Nigerian Civil War in Nigerian Literature," *Commonwealth Literature and the Modern World*, ed. Hena Maes-Jelinek (Bruxelles: Libraire Marcel Didier, 1975), p.108.

11 Kolawole Ogungbesan, "Politics and the African Writer," *African Studies Review* 17 (1974): p. 51

12 Philip Rogers, "Chinua Achebe's Poems of Regeneration," *Journal of Commonwealth Literature* 10. 3 (Apr. 1976), p. 2.

13 Philip Rogers, "Chinua Achebe's Poems of Regeneration," *Journal of Commonwealth Literature* 10. 3 (Apr. 1976), 2.

14 Philip Rogers, "Chinua Achebe's Poems of Regeneration," *ournal of Commonwealth Literature* 10. 3 (Apr. 1976), p. 9.

15 Philip Rogers, "Chinua Achebe's Poems of Regeneration," *Journal of Commonwealth Literature* 10. 3 (Apr. 1976), 6.

16 Philip Rogers, "Chinua Achebe's Poems of Regeneration," *Journal of Commonwealth Literature* 10. 3 (Apr. 1976), 6.

17 Philip Rogers, "Chinua Achebe's Poems of Regeneration," *Journal of Commonwealth Literature* 10. 3 (Apr. 1976), p. 7.

18 Bernth Lindfors, et al., p. 22.

19 Kolawole Ogungbesan, p. 46.

20 Wole Soyinka, "The Writer in a Modern African State," *The Writer in Modern Africa*, ed. by Per Wästberg, p. 21.

21 Chinua Achebe, "Interview by Robert Serumaga," *African Writers Talking*, p. 13.

22 Neal Ascherson's comment mentioned earlier about reckless use of power aptly describes the kind of sensibility that engenders this sort of abuse: "Betrayal," *New York Review of Books* 35. 3 (Mar. 3, 1988), 3.

23 Bernth Lindfors, et al., pp. 9-10.

24 Nadine Gordimer, "A Tyranny of Clowns," *The New York Times Book Review* (Feb. 21, 1988), p. 26.

25 Nadine Gordimer, "A Tyranny of Clowns," *The New York Times Book Review* (Feb. 21, 1988), p. 26..(The old man's analysis covers a wider area of Achebe's views on the role of the writer. See An*thills of the Savannah*, pp. 123-5).

26 Chinua Achebe, "The Black Writer's Burden," *Présence Africaine* 31 (1966), p. 138.

27 Chinua Achebe, "The Black Writer's Burden," *Présence Africaine* 31 (1966) p. 139.

28 David Murphy, *The Silent Watchdog: the Press in Local Politics*, p. 11.

Conclusion

[1] Chinua Achebe, "The Novelist as Teacher," *Morning Yet on Creation Day*, pp. 44.

[2] Chinua Achebe, "The Novelist as Teacher," *Morning Yet on Creation Day*, P. 45.

[3] Bernth Lindfors, et al., p. 7.

[4] Rogers Philip, "Chinua Achebe's Poems of Regeneration," p. 5.

[5] Achebe's vision of the sort of artist/critic that the contemporary society needs as against the one that had always operated in traditional society is compounded by the fascist oriented governments within which such contemporary artists have to work. Modern societies in which the freedom of criticism as functioned in traditional societies is curtailed by blatant intimidations and draconian decrees, and often physical incarcerations: "Mr Achebe said his relations with authorities are strained.He went home in December to accept an honorary doctorate from the state university at Lagos, for example; the ceremony was abruptly called off. . . . 'It's risky and dangerous, this kind of love-hate relationship with authorities,' he said, 'but I really have no choice in the matter. I would be very, very sad to have to live in Europe or America [exile].'" Kim Heron, "A Risky and Dangerous Relationship," *The New York Times* (Feb. 21, 1988), p. 26.

[6] Kim Heron, "A Risky and Dangerous Relationship,"*The New York Times* (Feb. 21, 1988), p. 26.

[7] Ngugi Wa Thiong'o, "The Writer in a Changing Society," *Homecoming: Essays on African and Caribbean Literature, Culture and Politics*, (London: Heinemann, 1972), p. 47.

[8] Ngugi Wa Thiong'o, "Chinua Achebe: A Man of the People," *Homecoming: Essays on African and Caribbean Literature, Culture and Politics*, p. 52.

[9] Ngugi Wa Thiong'o, "Chinua Achebe: *A Man of the People*," *Homecoming: Essays on African and Caribbean Literature, Culture and Politics*, p. 54.

Bibliography

Primary Sources

Achebe, Chinua. *Anthills of the Savannah*. London: Heinemann, 1987.
_____*Arrow of God*. 1964. London: Heinemann, 1978.
_____ *Beware Soul Brother*. (First published by Nwankwo-Ifejika, Nigeria: 1971).London: Heinemann, 1972.
_____*Girls at War and Other Stories*. London: Heinemann, 1972.
_____ *A Man of the People*. 1966. London: Heinemann, 1967.
_____ *No Longer at Ease*. 1960. London: Heinemann, 1969.
_____*Things Fall Apart*. 1958. London: Heinemann, 1963.

Secondary Sources
Books

Achebe, Chinua. *Morning Yet on Creation Day*. London: Heinemann, 1975.
_____*The Trouble with Nigeria*. London: Heinemann, 1984. (First published by Fourth Dimension Publishing Co., Enugu, Nigeria in 1983).
Ademola, Frances, ed. *Reflections: Nigerian Prose and Verse*. Lagos: African University Press, 1962.
Awoonor, Kofi. *The Breast of the Earth*. New York: Anchor Press, 1976.
Carroll, David. *Chinua Achebe*. New York: St Martin's Press, 1980.
Cartey, Wilfred. *Whispers From a Continent: the Literature of Contemporary Black Africa*. 1969. London: Heinemann, 1971.
Cary, Joyce. *Mister Johnson*. 1939. Carfax Edition. London: Michael Joseph, 1961.

Cook, David. *African Literature: A Critical View.* London: Longman, 1977.
Dathorne, O. R. *The Black Mind.* Minneapolis: University of Minnesota Press, 1974.
Duerden, Dennis, and Cosmo Pieterse, eds. *African Writers Talking.* London: Heinemann, 1972.
Echeruo, Michael J. C. *Joyce Cary and the Novel of Africa.* London: Longmans, 1973.
Egudu, R.N.*Modern African Poetry and the African Predicament.* London: Macmillan, 1971.
Ferres, John H. and Martin Tucker, eds and comps. *Modern Commonwealth Literature.* New York: Frederick Ungar Publ., 1977.
Gakwandi, Shatto Arthur. *The Novel and Contemporary Experience in Africa.* New York: Africana Publishing Company, 1977.
Heywood Christopher, ed. *Perspectives on African Literature.* London: Heinemann,1971.
Killam, G.D., ed. *African Writers on African Writing.* Evanston: Northwestern University Press, 1973.
_____Novels of Chinua Achebe. London: Heinemann, 1969.
King, Bruce, ed. *Introduction to Nigerian Literature.* 1971. New York: Africana, 1972.
King, Bruce, and Kolawole Ogungbesan, eds. *A Celebration of Black and African Writing.* Zaria: Ahmadu Bello UP and Oxford UP, 1975.
Larson, Charles R. The Emergence of African Fiction. Rev. ed. Bloomington: Indiana University Press, 1972 .
Lindfors, Bernth, et al., eds. *Palaver: Interviews with Five African Writers in Texas.* Texas: African and Afro-American Research Institute, 1972.
McEwan, Neil. *Africa and the Novel.* London: McMillan, 1983.
McLeod, A.L, ed.*African Literature in English: Development and Identity.*Philadelphia: African Studies Association: Literature in English Group, 1981.

Moore, Gerald. *The Chosen Tongue*. London: Longmans, 1969.
_____*Seven African Writers*. Oxford, England: Oxford University Press, 1962.
Moore, Gerald, and Ulli Beier, eds. *Modern Poetry from Africa*. 1963 Middlesex: Penguin, 1970 (rev.and rept.ed).
Nazareth, Peter.*An African View of Literature*. 1972 Illinois: Northwestern University Press, 1974.
Palmer, Eustace. An *Introduction to the African Novel*. London: Heinemann, 1972.
Ravenscroft, Arthur.*Chinua Achebe*. ed.by Ian Scott-Kilvert, London: Longmans, 1969.
Roscoe, Adrian A. *Mother is Gold: A Study in West African Literature*. Cambridge, England: Cambridge University Press, 1971.
Smith, Rowland, ed.*Exile and Tradition*. New York: Africana Publishing Company, 1976.
Soyinka, Wole. *Myth, Literature and the African World*. London: Cambridge University Press, 1976.
Taiwo, Oladele. *Culture and the Nigerian Novel*. New York: St Martin's press, 1976.
Walsh, William. *Commonwealth Literature*. Oxford:Oxford University Press, 1973.
Walshe, R.D. ed. *Speaking of Writing*. Sydney: Reed Education, 1975.
Wästberg, Per, ed. *The Writer in Modern Africa*: African - Scandinavian Writers' Conference, Stockholm, 1967. New York: Africana, 1969.
Wa Thiong'o, Ngugi. *Homecoming: Essays on African and Caribbean Literature, Culture and Politics*. London: Heinemann, 1972.
Zell, M. Hans, and Silver, Helene, eds. A Readers Guide to African Literature. London: Heinemann, 1972.

Articles and Reviews

Achebe, Chinua. "Africa and Her Writers." *Massachussetts Review* 14 (1973): 617-29.
_____ "The Black Writer's Burden." *Présence Africaine* 31 (1966): 135-40.
_____ "The Novelist as Teacher." *African Writers on African Writing* ed. Killam, G.D.Evanston: Northwestern UP, 1973. 1-4.
_____ *"The Role of the Writer in a New Nation."* Killam 7-13.
_____ "Where Angels Fear to Tread." Killam 4-7.
Anber, Paul. "Modernisation and Political Disintegration: Nigeria and the Ibos." *Journal of Modern African Studies* 5 (1967): 163-79.
Ascherson, Neal. "Betrayal." Rev.of *Anthills of the Savannah* by Chinua Achebe. New York Book Review 3 Mar. 1988: 3-6.
Barnes, Hugh. "Turns of the Screw." Rev. of *Things Fall Apart* by Chinua Achebe. *London Review of Books* 7 Aug. 1986: 24-6.
Beckmann, Susan. "Language as Cultural Identity in Achebe, Ihimaera, Laurence and Atwood."World Literature Written in English 20.1 (1981): 117-34.
Beier, Ulli. "The Conflict of Cultures: in West African Poetry." *Black Orpheus* 1 (1957): 17-21.
_____ "Ibo and Yoruba Arts: a Comparison." *Black Orpheu*s 8 (c1960): 46-58.
Cairns, P. "Style, Structure and the Status of Language in Chinua Achebe's*Things Fall Apart* and *Arrow of God." World Literature Written in English* 25.1 (1985): 1-9.
Chukwukere, B. I. "The Problem of Language in African Creative Writing." *African Literature Today* 3 (1969): 15-26.
De Graft, J.C. "Roots in African Drama and Theatre." *African Literature Today* 8 (1976): 1-25.
Ekwensi, Cyprain. "African Literature." *Nigerian Magazine* 83 (1964): 294-9.
Emenyonu, Ernest. "African Literature: What Does it Take to be Its Critic?" *African Literature Today* 5 (1971): 1-11.

Etherton, Michael. "Trends in African Theatre." *African Literature Today* 10 (1979): 57-85.

Frank, Katherine. "Feminist Criticism and the African Novel." *African Literature Today* 14 (1984): 34-48.

Gordimer, Nadine. "A Tyranny of Clowns." Rev. of *Anthills of the Savannah* by Chinua Achebe. *New York Times Book Review* 21 Feb. 1988: 1-26.

Gowda, H.H. Anniah. "The Novels of Chinua Achebe." *The Literary Half-Yearly* 14.2 (1973): 3-9.

Griffiths, Gareth. "Language and Action in the Novels of Chinua Achebe." *African Literature Today* 5 (1971): 88-105.

Gugelberger, M.Georg. "Blake, Neruda, Ngugi Wa Thiong'o: Issues in Third World Literature."*Comparative Literature Studies* 21.4 (1984): 462-82.

Hale, Thomas. "Africa and the West: Close Encounters of a Literary Kind." *Comparative Literature Studies* 20.3 (1983): 261-75.

_____"Enter the Iconoclast: Buchi Emecheta and the Igbo Culture." *Commonwealth* 7.2 (1985): 83-94.

Heron, Kim. "A Risky and Dangerous Relationship." *New York Times Book Review* 21 Feb. 1988: 26.

Ikiddeh, Ime. Foreword. *Homecoming: Essays on African and Caribbean Literature, Culture and Politics.* by Ngugi Wa Thiong'o. London: Heinemann, 1972.

Ilogu, Edmund. "Chritianity and Ibo Traditional Religion." *Nigerian Magazine* 83 (1964): 304-8.

Irele, Abiola. "Negritude or Black Cultural Nationalism." *The Journal of Modern African Studies* 3.3 (1965): 321-48.

_____"Negritude - Literature and Ideology." *The Journal of Modern African Studies* 3.4 (1965): 499-526.

Iyasere, O. Solomon. "Art, a Simulcrum of Reality - Problems in the Criticism of African Literature." The *Journal of Modern African Studies* 11 (1973): 447-55.

_____"African Critics on African Literature: a Study in Misplaced Hostility." *African Literature Today* 7 (1975): 21-7.

_____ "African Oral Tradition - Criticism as a Performance: a Ritual." *African Literature Today* 11 (1980): 169-74.

_____ "Cultural Formalism and the Criticism of Modern African Literature." *Journal of Modern African Studies* 14 (1976): 322-30.

_____ "Oral Tradition in the Criticism of African Literature." Journal of Modern African Studies 13.1 (1975): 107-19.

_____ Rev. of The Emergence of African Fiction, by Charles Larson.*Journal of Modern African Studies* 12 (1974): 160-3.

_____ "The Liberation of African Literature - a Re-evaluation of the Socio-Cultural Approach.".*The Conch* 5.1-2 (1973): 1-10.

Izevbaye, Dan."Issues in the Reassessment of the African Novel." *African Literature Today* 10 (1979): 7-31.

_____ "The State of Criticism in African Literature." *African Literature Today* 7 (1975): 1-19.

Jabbi, Bu-Buakei. "Influence and Originality in African Writing." *African Literature Today* 10 (1979): 107-23.

_____ "Myth and Ritual in Arrow of God." *African Literature Today* 11 (1980): 130-48.

Janmohamed, Abdul."Sophisticated Primitivism: the Syncretism of Oral and Literate Modes in Achebe's *Things Fall Apart.*" *Ariel* 15.4 (1984):19-39.

Johnson, C. Alex."Creative Tension in West African Drama in English: the Linguistic Dimension".*World Literature Written in English* 24.1 (1984): 64-78.

Jones, D. Eldred. "Chinua Achebe." Rev. of *Beware Soul Brother* by Chinua Achebe. *African Literature Today* 6 (1973): 181-2.

July, W. Robert. "African Personality: African Literature and the African Personality." *Black Orpheus* 14 (1964): 33-45.

King, Bruce."The Revised *Arrow of God.*" *African Literature Today* 13 (1983): 69-78.

Kuesgen, Reinhardt "Conrad and Achebe: Aspects of the Novel." *World Literature Written in English* 24.1 (1984): 27-33.

Lamb, Jonathan. "Problems of Originality: or, Beware of Pakeha baring Guilts." *Landfall* 40.3 (1986): 352-8.

Lindfors, Bernth."The Blindmen and the Elephant." *African Literature Today* 7 (1975): 53-64.

_____"The Palmoil with which Achebe's Words are Eaten." *African Literature Today* 1 (1969): 2-19. (Originally published in *Nigeria Magazine*, June 1964).

_____"Popular Literature for an African Elite." *Journal of Modern African Studies* 12 (1974): 471-86.

Maduka, T. Chukwudi. "The African Writer and the Drama of Social Change." *Ariel* 12.3 (1981): 5-18.

Moore, Gerald."Chinua Achebe: Nostalgia and Realism." *Seven AfricanWriters*, by Gerald Moore. London: Oxford UP, 1962. 58-72.

Mortty, G. Adali. Rev.of *Things Fall Apart* by Chinua Achebe. *Black Orpheus* 6 (1959): 48-50.

Mphahlele, Ezekiel. "The Language of African Literature." *Harvard Educational Review* 34.2 (1964): 298-306.

Neill, Michael. "Coming Home: Teaching the Post-Colonial Novel." *Islands* 2 (1985): 38-53.

Niven, Alastair. "The Family in Modern African Literature." *Ariel* 12.3 (1981): 81-91.

Nwoga, D.I. "Modern African Poetry: the Domestication of a Tradition." *African Literature Today* 10 (1979): 33-56.

Obiechina, E.N. "Cultural Nationalism in Modern African Creative Literature." *African Literature Today* 1 (1969): 24-35.

_____Problem of Language in African Writing: the Example of the Novel." *The Conch* 5.1-2 (1973): 11-28.

O'Flinn, J.P. "Towards a Sociology of the Nigerian Novel." *African Literature Today* 7 (1975): 34-52.

Ogu, Julius N. "The Concept of Madness in Chinua Achebe's Writings." *Journal of Commonwealth Literature* 18.1 (1983): 48-54.

Ogude, S.E. "Slavery and the African Imagination: a Critical Perspective." *World Literature Today* 55 (1981): 21-5.

Ogungbesan, Kolawole. "Politics and the African Writer." *African Studies Review* 17 (1974): 43-53.

Oko, Emelia Aseme. "The Historical Novel of Africa: a Sociological Approach to Achebe's *Things Fall Apart* and *Arrow of God*." *The Conch* 6.1&2 (1974): 15-46.

Okonkwo, Juliet. "The Missing Link in African Literature." *African Literature Today* 10 (1979): 86-105.

Okpewho, Isidore. "Comparatism and Separation in African Literature." *World Literature Today* 55 (1981): 25-31.

Onwubu, Chukwuemeka. "Ethnic Identity, Political Integration, and National Development: the Igbo Diaspora in Nigeria." *Journal of Modern African Studies* 13.3 (1975): 399-413.

Palmer, Eustace. "Novels and the Colonial Experience." Rev. of *The Colonial Encounter*, by M.M. Mahood. *African Literature Today* 10 (1979): 248-52.

Povey, John. "The Novels of Chinua Achebe." *Introduction to Nigerian Literature*, ed. Bruce King. 1971. New York: Africana, (1972): 97-112.

Priebe, Richard. "Escaping the Nightmare of History: the Development of Mythic Consciousness in West African Literature." *Ariel* 4.2 (1973): 55-67.

Ravenscroft, Arthur. "African Literature V: Novels of Disillusion." *Journal of Commonwealth Literature* 3.6 (1969): 120-37.

_____"Conference on Commonwealth Literature: Aarhus, Denmark, 26-30 Apr. 1971." *Journal of Commonwealth Literature* 6.2 (1971): 126-9.

_____"The Nigerian Civil War in Nigerian Literature." *Commonwealth Literature and the Modern World* ed. Hena Maes-Jelinek.Bruxelles: Librairie Marcel Didier, 1975.

Riddy, Felicity. "Language as a Theme in No Longer at Ease." *Journal of Commonwealth Literature* 5.9 (Jul. 1970): 38-47.

Riemenschneider, Dieter. "The Biafran War in Nigerian Literature." *Journal of Commonwealth Literature* 18.1 (1983): 55

Rogers, Philip. "Chinua Achebe's Poems of Regeneration." *Journal of Commonwealth Literature* 10.3 (1976): 1-9.

Sabor, Peter. "Palm-wine and Drinkards: African Literature and Its Critics." *Ariel* 12.3 (1981): 113-25.

Schipper, Mineke. "Eurocentrism and Criticism: Reflections on the Study of Literature in Past and Present." *World Literature Written in English* 24.1 (1984): 16-27.

Speed, Diane. Rev. of *Things Fall Apart* by Chinua Achebe. *Black Orpheus* 5 (May 1959): 52.

Stock, A. G. "Yeats and Achebe." *Journal of Commonwealth Literature* 3.5 (1968): 105-11.

Stuart, Donald. "African Literature III: the Modern Writer in His Context." *Journal of Commonwealth Literature* 4 (1967): 113-29.

Wa Thiong'o, Ngugi. "A Kind of Homecoming." *Homecoming: Essays on African and Caribbean Literature, Culture and Politics*. London: Heinemann, 1972. 81-95.

_____ "Chinua Achebe: A Man of the People." *Homecoming: Essays on African and Caribbean Literature, Culture and Politics*. London: Heinemann, 1972. 51-4.

_____ "The Writer and His Past." *Homecoming: Essays on African and Caribbean Literature, Culture and Politics*. London: Heinemann, 1972. 39-46.

____ "The Writer in a Changing Society." *Homecoming: Essays on African and Caribbean Literature, Culture and Politics*. London: Heinemann, 1972.47-50.

Wattie, Nelson. "The Community as Protagonist in the Novels of Chinua Achebe and Witi Ihimaera." *Individual and Community in Commonwealth Literature* ed. Daniel Massa. Malta: University Press, 1979. 69-74.

Webb, Hugh. "The African Historical Novel and the Way Forward." *African Literature Today* 11 (1980): 24-38.

Wren, M. Robert. "The Indigenization of English: Rhetoric in Modern Nigerian Literature." *Black Orpheus* 3.4 (1976): 44-55.

Wright, Edgar. "African Literature I: Problems of Criticism." *The Journal of Commonwealth Literature* 2 (1966): 103-12.

Theses

Ogba, Kalu. Folkways in Chinua Achebe's Novels. Diss. University of Texas at Austin, Ph.D. 1981.Ann Arbor: UMI, 1982. 82-17961.

Ogbonnaya, Anthonia Chinyere. Chinua Achebe and the Igbo World View. Diss. University of Wisconsin Madison, Ph.D. 1984. Ann Arbor: UMI, 1982. 84 - 13267.

www.ingramcontent.com/pod-product-compliance
Lightning Source LLC
Chambersburg PA
CBHW061958220426
43662CB00011B/1731